# st○pwatch

Student's Book
& Workbook

**2**

Viviane Kirmeliene

CB053058

Richmond

58 St Aldates
Oxford
OX1 1ST
United Kingdom

**Publisher:** *Justine Piekarowicz*
**Editorial Team:** *Daniel Altamirano, Suzanne Guerrero, Kimberly MacCurdy, Joep van der Werff*
**Art and Design Coordinators:** *Jaime Angeles, Karla Avila*
**Design:** *Jaime Angeles, Karla Avila*
**Layout:** *Erick López, Daniel Mejia*
**Pre-Press Coordinator:** *Daniel Santillán*
**Pre-Press Team:** *Susana Alcántara, Virginia Arroyo, Daniel Santillán*
**Cover Design:** *Karla Avila*
Cover Photograph: © *Thinkstock: IPGGutenbergUKLtd* (Young Woman Swimming in Pool)

**Illustrations:** Karla Avila p. 125, Tomas Benitez p. 28, 29, 32; Berenice Muñiz p. 72; Ismael Vázquez p. 16, 24, 30, 40, 44, 53, 84, 110, 114, 127, 151

**Photos:** © **Brooke Sabin:** p. 91 (storyteller, bottom);
© **Little, Brown and Company:** p. 84, 89 (I Am Malala);
© **Penguin Random House:** p. 84, 88 (The Diary of a Young Girl);
© **Shutterstock:** TonyV3112 p. 10 (top left), Paolo Bona p. 23 (bottom left), Xuanhuongho p. 27 (motorcycles in Ho Chi Minh City), Vivek Agrawal p. 30 (center), Thinglass p. 35 (map), Dan Kitwood p. 35 (top left), Denys Prykhodov p. 42, 58, 141 (Ipad), Radu Bercan p. 44 (top left), Tofudevil p. 48 (cosplayers), Tle 411 p. 48 (dog), Cowardlion p. 49 (top right), Featureflash p. 54 (Hugh Jackman), s_bukley p. 54 (Emma Watson), Tinseltown p. 54 (Jim Parsons), Iakov Filimonov p. 62, Andrew F. Kazmierski p. 70 (street vendor), Oscity p. 70 (downtown Aspen), John Wollwerth p. 70 (aquarium), Bankoo p. 74 (Great Wall of China), Andrey Bayda p. 74 (beach), Fotokon p. 74 (restaurant), Pierdelune p. 75 (top right), Chuck Wagner p. 77 (parade), Pavel L Photo and Video p. 77 (dancers), Fotoluminate LLC p. 77 (jazz band), Littleny p. 80 (street market), Idome p. 80 (Macau historic center), Tupungato p. 80 (museum), Panom p. 84 (Wolverine), J. Simunek p. 84, 95 (The Hobbit), MAC1 p. 86 (air plane, left), Catwalker p. 87 (stamp), Patryk Kosmider p. 89 (concentration camp), Catwalker p. 89 (stamp), kavalenkava volha p. 89 (view of Amsterdam), rook76 p. 95 (bottom), Aleksandar Todorovic p. 104 (Masai women, top left), Franco Volpato p. 104 (African children), Photo.ua p. 111 (carrousel), DonLand p. 118 (beach resort, top right), Boykov p. 119 (dancers, top right), Featureflash p. 134, Paul Wishart p. 145 (Louvre), Sira Anamwong p. 145 (Arc de Triomphe), tristan tan p. 152 (stamp); Cylonphoto p. 153 (voluntary youth organization);
© **Joep van der Werff:** p. 84 (Harry Potter and the Chamber of Secrets; An Abundance of Katherines; Charlie and the Chocolate Factory), p. 86 (Roald Dahl books);
© **Skokloster Castle/Open Image Archive:** p. 55;
© **Wikipedia:** p. 149 (portrait), p. 149 (signature)
Images used under license from © **Shutterstock.com** and © **Thinkstock.com**.

All rights reserved. No part of this work may be reproduced, stored in a retrieval system or transmitted in any form or by any means without prior written permission from the Publisher.

Richmond publications may contain links to third party websites or apps. We have no control over the content of these websites or apps, which may change frequently, and we are not responsible for the content or the way it may be used with our materials. Teachers and students are advised to exercise discretion when accessing the links.

The Publisher has made every effort to trace the owner of copyright material; however, the Publisher will correct any involuntary omission at the earliest opportunity.

**Impressão e acabamento:** Bercrom Gráfica e Editora
**Lote:** 768.445
**Cód.:** 292712442

---

Dados Internacionais de Catalogação na Publicação (CIP)
(Câmara Brasileira do Livro, SP, Brasil)

Kirmeliene, Viviane
    Stopwatch 2 : student's book & workbook / Viviane Kirmeliene. — São Paulo : Moderna, 2018.

    1. Inglês - Estudo e ensino I. Título.

17-09951                                      CDD-420.7

Índices para catálogo sistemático:
1. Inglês : Estudo e ensino     420.7

**ISBN 978-85-16-10898-4**

*All rights reserved.*
No part of this work may be reproduced, stored in a retrieval system or transmitted in any form, electronic, mechanical, photocopying or otherwise without the prior permission in writing of the copyright holders.

**RICHMOND**
**SANTILLANA EDUCAÇÃO LTDA.**
Rua Padre Adelino, 758 – 3º andar – Belenzinho
São Paulo – SP – Brasil – CEP 03303-904
www.richmond.com.br
2022
Printed in Brazil

# Contents

## Student's Book

- 4 — Scope and Sequence
- 7 — Unit 0 What are stereotypes?
- 13 — Unit 1 Why are sports important?
- 27 — Unit 2 How do you get around?
- 41 — Unit 3 What makes a good friend?
- 55 — Unit 4 What do we eat?
- 69 — Unit 5 Why do we need a vacation?
- 83 — Unit 6 What's your story?
- 97 — Unit 7 How do we contribute?
- 111 — Unit 8 How do we spend our free time?

## Workbook

- 126 — Unit 1
- 130 — Unit 2
- 134 — Unit 3
- 138 — Unit 4
- 142 — Unit 5
- 146 — Unit 6
- 150 — Unit 7
- 154 — Unit 8

- 158 — Just for Fun Answer Key
- 159 — Grammar Reference
- 168 — Verb List

# Scope and Sequence

| Unit | Vocabulary | Grammar | Skills |
|---|---|---|---|
| **0** What are stereotypes? | **Review:** countries, nationalities, common verbs | Verb *be*; *There is / are;* Present continuous; Present simple; Prepositions of place: *at, behind, in, in front of, on, under* | **Reading:** Reading e-mails |
| **1** Why are sports important? | **Sports:** baseball, basketball, cricket, cycling, football, rugby, soccer, swimming, tennis, table tennis<br>**Adjectives:** active, big, dangerous, expensive, fast, heavy, modern, old, popular, strong, tall | Comparative and superlative adjectives | **Reading:** Knowing when to look up words<br>**Writing:** Expressing opinions<br>**Project:** Writing a sports manual |
| **2** How do you get around? | **Places in a City:** bank, coffee shop, convenience store, drugstore, mall, park, school, supermarket<br>**Transportation:** bike, bus, car, motorcycle, plane, subway, train | Imperatives; Irregular comparative and superlative adjectives | **Listening:** Following directions on a map<br>**Reading:** Identifying the objective of a text<br>**Project:** Writing a proposal |
| **3** What makes a good friend? | **Physical Description:** blond, braces, chubby, glasses, long, medium height, medium weight, short, thin<br>**Personality:** funny, intelligent, kind, outgoing, rude, serious, shy | Present simple; Present continuous | **Listening:** Identifying speaker's attitude<br>**Writing:** Completing a form<br>**Project:** Making a self-care kit |
| **4** What do we eat? | **Food and Drinks:** apple, banana, beans, beef, bread, broccoli, butter, carrot, cheese, chicken, egg, fish, juice, milk, onions, oranges, pasta, rice, soda, water | Countable and uncountable nouns; Quantifiers: *some, any* | **Reading:** Identifying main ideas<br>**Speaking:** Recommending a restaurant<br>**Project:** Writing a healthy menu |

| Unit | Vocabulary | Grammar | Skills |
|---|---|---|---|
| **5** Why do we need a vacation? | **Tourist Attractions:** amusement park, aquarium, art museum, beach, historic center, mountains, street market, zoo<br>**Adjectives:** beautiful, boring, crowded, fun, great, noisy, terrible | Verb *be: was, were* | **Listening:** Predicting the information<br>**Writing:** Making a vacation scrapbook<br>**Project:** Making a podcast |
| **6** What's your story? | **Movie and Book Genres:** autobiography, children's book, fantasy, romance, action, animated, comedy, science fiction<br>**Adjectives:** boring, funny, sad, interesting, inspirational<br>**Irregular Verbs:** found, made, met, saw, went, wrote | Past simple | **Listening:** Identifying sequence in a narrative<br>**Writing:** Connecting ideas in a past-tense text<br>**Project:** Making a timeline |
| **7** How do we contribute? | **Professions:** artist, journalist, nurse, scientist, social worker<br>**Workplaces:** community center, hospital, laboratory, office, studio | Past simple | **Reading:** Identifying the purpose: *persuade, inform, entertain*<br>**Speaking:** Talking about a hero based on prompts<br>**Project:** Solving a problem in the community |
| **8** How do we spend our free time? | **Chores and Free-time Activities:** clean (your) room, do the dishes, do homework, go to the park, hang out with friends, play video games, take out the trash, walk the dog, watch a movie<br>**Emotions:** angry, bored, excited, happy, nervous, sad, scared, tired | *Have to;*<br>Future: *going to* | **Reading:** Reading for specific information<br>**Speaking:** Inviting, accepting and rejecting an invitation<br>**Project:** Carrying out and presenting a survey |

# Unit 0

**Yellow Mango, Red Tropics Juice for the Perfect Family**

**1** **Look and write *there is* or *there are*.**

(0) __There is__ a "perfect family" in the picture. (1) _____ two children: a boy and a girl. (2) _____ a mother and (3) _____ a father. They are all wearing white clothes. They are eating dinner. (4) _____ a chicken and (5) _____ glasses with juice. The father is cutting the chicken.

**2** **Label the pictures. What are they advertising?**

🖌 a beach vacation    music    shampoo

_____    _____    _____

3 Answer the questions about the people on page 8.

0. Are the people happy?   Yes, they are.
1. Are they old?   _____
2. Are they ordinary people?   _____
3. Are they rich?   _____

**Stop and Think!** How does advertising use stereotypes?

4 Write the professions.

business people   dancer   ~~math student~~   nurse   scientists   truck driver

0. math student

1. _____

2. _____

3. _____

4. _____

5. _____

5 🎧¹ Write questions and answers. Then listen and check your answers.

0. (write on the board) What is the math student doing?   She is writing on the board.
1. (complete a report) _____
2. (work in the lab) _____
3. (talk to her family) _____
4. (have a meeting) _____
5. (dance ballet) _____

1. 

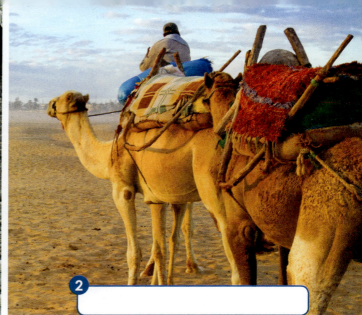
2. 

3. 

4. 

**6  Look and label the countries.**

🖌 China   France   India   Italy
Kenya   Mexico   Morocco
United States

**7  Read and circle the correct option.**

0. Three tourists are sitting **(in)/ under** a tricycle called a rickshaw.
1. There are two camels walking in the desert. A man is sitting **in / on** one of the animals.
2. This woman has a *baguette,* typical bread from her country. We can see the Eiffel Tower **behind / in front of** her.
3. The mariachi singer lives **at / in** a small town. He has a big sombrero hat **in / on** his head.

**8  Correct the underlined words.**

0. _Americans_ United States like hamburgers.
1. _____ People in Italian eat pizza and spaghetti.
2. _____ Koalas are Australia animals.
3. _____ There are many camels in Northern African.
4. _____ Japan women wear kimonos.

**Glossary**

**American:** a person who is born or lives in the United States; or a person who is born or lives in North, Central or South America

**9** **Read and circle *T* (True) or *F* (False).**

1. All people in Morocco live in the desert.     T    F
2. French people eat *baguettes*.     T    F
3. All French people visit the Eiffel Tower on vacation.     T    F
4. Muslim girls in the hotel wear a special swimsuit.     T    F

 **Stop and Think!**    Is it OK to make generalizations about groups of people?

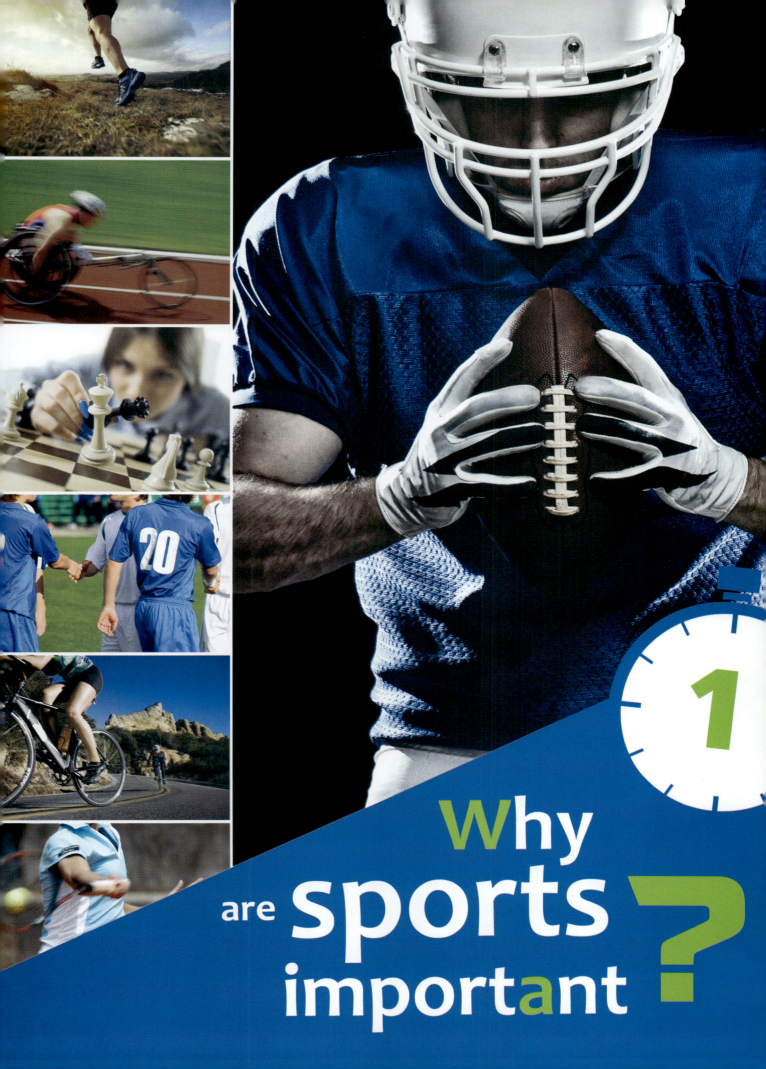

# Why are sports important?

1

# Vocabulary

SPECTATOR SPORTS,

**1** 🎧² **Listen and number five sports.**

- ☐ baseball
- ☐ football
- ☐ soccer
- ☐ basketball
- ☐ ice hockey
- ☐ table tennis
- ☐ cricket
- ☐ rugby
- ☐ tennis

**2** 🎧³ **Listen and write the sports in the map.**

1. baseball
2. ice hockey
3. cricket
4. rugby
5. table tennis

**3 Classify the words.**

- basketball
- exercise
- judo
- run
- swim
- tennis

Canada:

United States: football, basketball

Cuba:

Brazil: volleyball

| Do | Play | Verb |
|---|---|---|
| In one place, individual | A team sport, a ball sport | An individual activity |
| I _do karate._ | We _play soccer._ | He _rides a bike._ |
| He does _____ | She plays _____ | They _____ |
| She does _____ | I play _____ | You _____ |

# SIMPLIFIED

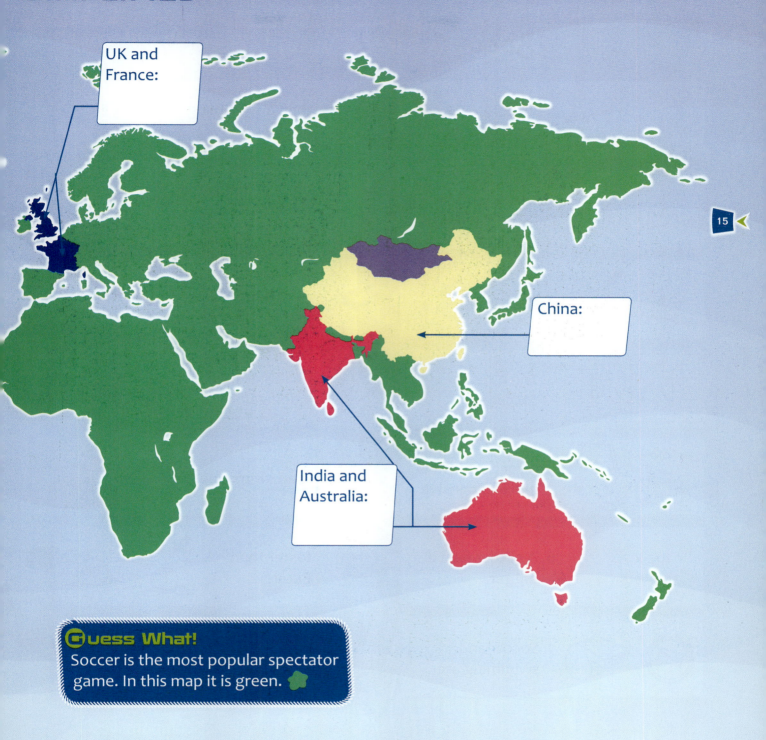

UK and France:

China:

India and Australia:

**Guess What!**
Soccer is the most popular spectator game. In this map it is green.

**4 Think Fast!** In your notebook, choose a sport and draw a symbol. A classmate guesses the sport.

baseball   basketball   cycling   golf   running   soccer
swimming   tennis   table tennis   volleyball

# Grammar

**1** Match the sentence pieces.

## Soccer vs. Swimming

1. Soccer is **more popular** — ___ **than** a swimming pool.  50 x 20 meters

2. The time for a soccer game is — 90 minutes — ___ **more complicated than** for swimming.

3. Mark swims — ___ **than** a swimming outfit.

4. The rules for soccer are — ___ **healthier than** video games!

5. A soccer outfit is **more expensive** — ___ **than** swimming.

6. A soccer field is **bigger** — 100 x 70 meters — ___ **faster than** Peter.

7. Soccer and swimming are — ___ **longer than** a basketball game. 48 minutes

**2** In your notebook, write the comparative forms.

fast   old   healthy   expensive   active   elegant

### Comparatives

adjectives
- 1 syllable: old → older than
- 2 + syllables: competitive → more competitive than

**3** Study the table and write *volleyball*, *basketball* or *tennis*.

|  | Volleyball | Basketball | Tennis |
|---|---|---|---|
| 1. Players on a team | 6 | 5 | 1 |
| 2. Court | 18 x 9 meters | 28 x 15 meters | 24 x 8 meters |
| 3. Invented | 1895 | 1891 | 1873-1881 |
| 4. Ball | 270 grams | 624 grams | 56 grams |

1. _____ has **the largest** team: 6 players.
2. A volleyball court is big, but a _____ court is **the biggest** of the three.
3. Volleyball is the **most modern** Olympic sport, and _____ is **the oldest**.
4. The tennis ball is **the lightest** and the _____ is **the heaviest**.

**4** Label the pictures with the superlative form.

1
(tall)

2
(strong)

3
(expensive)

4
(old)

### Superlatives

adjectives

| 1 syllable | 2 + syllables |
|---|---|
| fast | active |
| ↓ | ↓ |
| the fastest | the most active |

 **5 Think Fast!** In your notebook, write five adjectives in their three forms: regular, comparative and superlative.

# Reading & Writing

**1** Look at the pictures and read the title. Then circle *Yes* or *No*.

1. Is parkour an Olympic sport?    Yes    No
2. Do you need a uniform for parkour?    Yes    No
3. Do the kids use protection for their bodies?    Yes    No

## PARKOUR: Cool or <u>Dangerous</u>?

Parkour or "<u>free</u> running," is like an obstacle race. You get from point A to point B using your arms and legs. Parkour includes running, climbing and jumping. A person who <u>practices</u> parkour is a <u>traceur</u> (boy or man) or <u>traceuse</u> (girl or woman). Parkour is <u>originally</u> from France.

Some people don't want parkour in <u>public</u> areas. They say that parkour is too dangerous for kids. Obviously, *traceurs* need to <u>train</u> with a parkour group to learn all the techniques. Kids in big cities like the excitement of parkour, because it is spectacular. But they need to be very careful, because parkour can be dangerous!

▎A traceuse climbing over a wall

**2** Read the article. Then use red or green to circle the underlined words.

🟢 I understand this from the context.
🔴 I don't understand this from the context.

### Be Strategic!
When you find a difficult word, decide if it's important to look it up. Only use a dictionary when it's really necessary.

▶ Parkour training

**3 Complete the dictionary entries with two of the underlined words.**

_____ v, To receive instruction and practice for an activity, art or sport: *We need to _____ for the soccer competition.*

_____ n, A male participant in the activity or sport of parkour: *David Belle is considered the first _____.*

**4 Read the notes and write complete paragraphs.**

**Julia:**
- parkour not a team sport
- dangerous, can have accidents
- doesn't like
- aggressive

**Austin:**
- parkour = cool
- training → get stronger
- make friends
- training = fun
- take cool pictures!

Julia thinks that parkour is not a team sport. She thinks _____
_____
_____
_____

Austin says that parkour is a cool sport. He thinks _____
_____
_____
_____

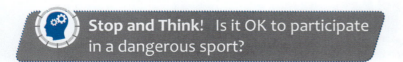

**Stop and Think!** Is it OK to participate in a dangerous sport?

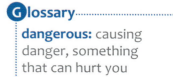

**G**lossary

**dangerous:** causing danger, something that can hurt you

# Culture

**1** Look at the pictures and discuss the questions.

  1. Who are riding bikes in the pictures?
  2. Do they ride bikes as a sport?
  3. How are they using their bikes?

**2** 🎧⁴ Listen to the rap and read along.

**3** Number the pictures.

### Bikes in Holland

I watch a program on TV
**Bikes** are a fascination
In Holland, as you can see
It is their transportation

There are bikes in the **rain** (1)
And bicycles in the **snow** (2)
Those bikes are everywhere you go!

A father **cycling** with his kids (3)
A grandmother **alone** (4)
The whole country is—I think:
A giant biking **zone**!

Businessmen ride bikes (5)
And businesswomen, too
I want to ride one; **how about you?**

### Glossary

**bike:** bicycle

**rain:** water that falls from the clouds

**snow:** frozen water that falls from the clouds in soft, white pieces

**cycling:** riding a bicycle

**alone:** not with another person

**zone:** area

**how about you?:** You, too?

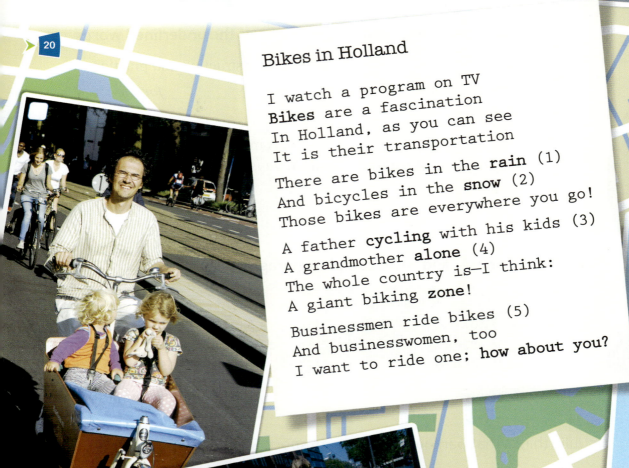

4 **Answer the questions.**
1. Are bikes more common in Holland or in your country? Why?
2. What is bike riding for you: playing with a toy, a sport or a form of transportation? Why?

**Stop and Think!** Is your city bicycle friendly?

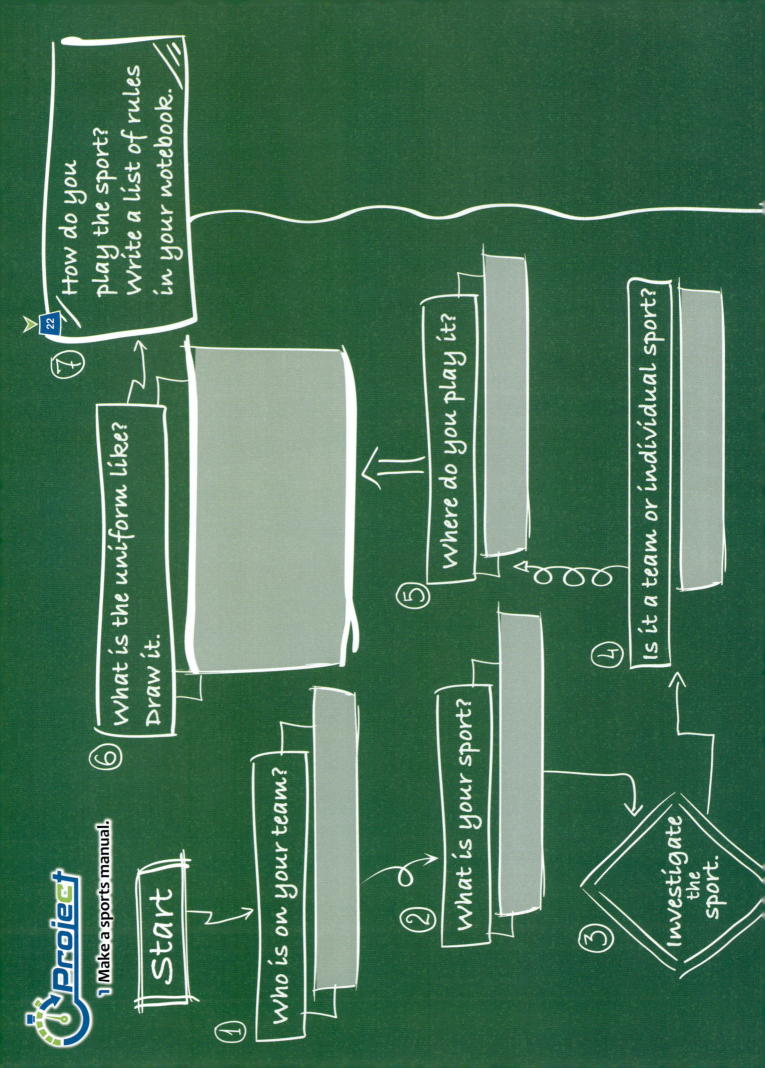

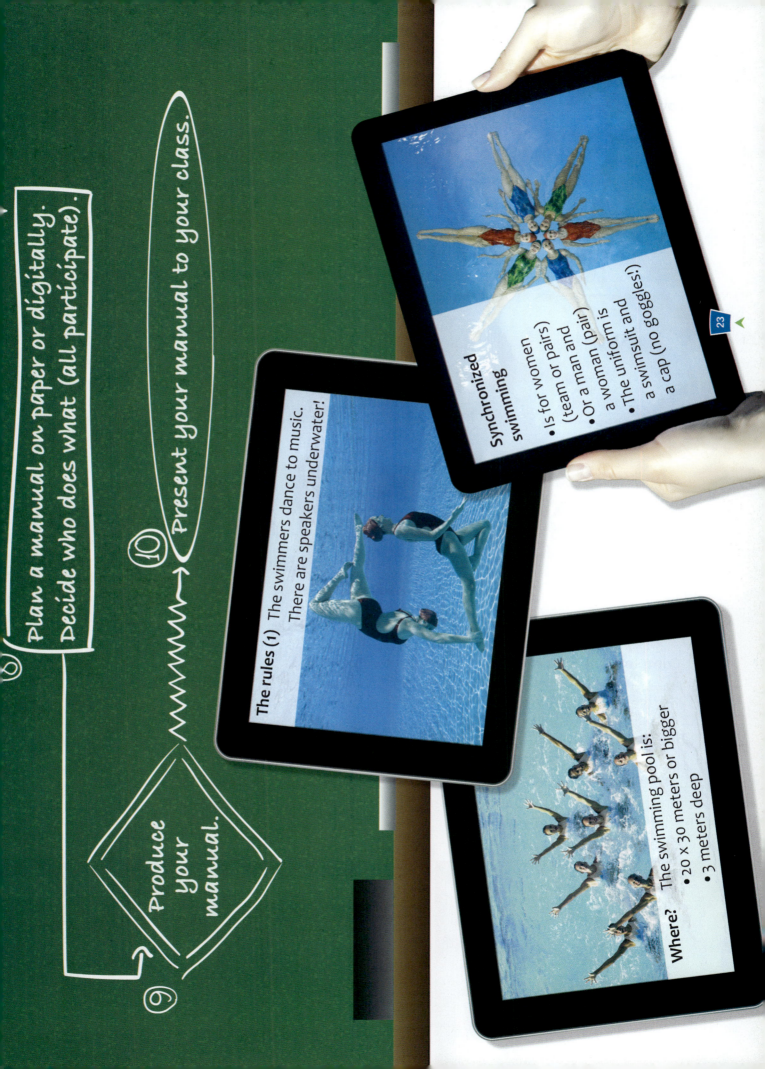

# Review

**1 Label the sports.**

_____     _____

_____     _____

_____     _____

**2 Complete the sentences using comparatives.**

I like basketball, but my brother Carlos prefers baseball. In basketball you run all the time. I think it's _____ (active) and _____ (fast) than baseball. The time for a baseball game is _____ (long) than the time for a basketball game. That's why basketball games on TV are _____ (popular) than baseball games.

I like to play baseball. I don't understand the rules of basketball. I think it's _____ (complicated) than baseball. For me, baseball is _____ (relaxing) than basketball. That's how I feel now. Maybe I'll change when I get _____ (old)!

3 Complete the table.

|  | adjective | comparative | superlative |
|---|---|---|---|
| regular, short | old | | |
| | big | | |
| | strong | | |
| regular, long | expensive | | |
| | exciting | | |

4 Match the sentence pieces. Write the number.

1. Larry is taller          ___ beautiful city in the country?
2. Dancing is more          ___ exciting than watching TV.
3. What is the most         ___ expensive than a tablet.
4. A laptop is more         ___ my sister.
5. I am heavier than        ___ than Frank.

5 Unscramble the sentences using the correct comparative or superlative form.

1. old (*comparative*) / the red car / is / the orange car / than
   _____

2. is / the red car / big (*superlative*) / of the three
   _____

3. the red / expensive (*comparative*) / blue car / car is / than the
   _____

4. heavy (*superlative*) of / car #1 / the three / is
   _____

5. modern (*comparative*) than / the blue / car is / the orange car
   _____

# Just for Fun

**1 Look and match.**

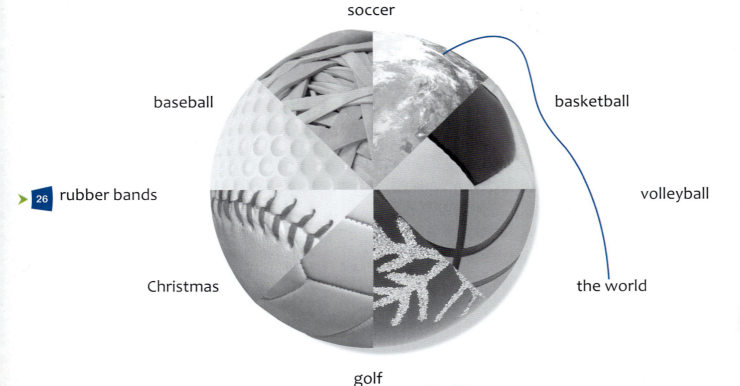

soccer
baseball
basketball
rubber bands
volleyball
Christmas
the world
golf

**2 Write the number.**

1. What animal is excellent at baseball?     ____ Catch you later!
2. What did the baseball glove say to the ball?     ____ A bat.
3. What sport do insects like?     ____ She runs away from the ball!
4. Why can't Cinderella play volleyball?     ____ Cricket.

**3 Write the answers.**

**Down** ↓

1. A woman or girl who practices parkour
2. Another word for ping-pong

**Across** →

3. A popular activity in Holland
4. Heavy, heavier, …
5. The topic of this unit

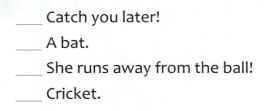

**4 Follow the instructions.**

Copy the dots in your notebook. Connect the nine dots with four straight lines. Don't take your pencil off the paper.

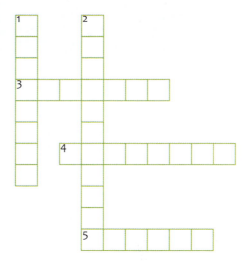

# 2
## How do you get around?

**1** 🎧⁵ **Listen and number the places on the map.**

**2 Read and mark (✓) the correct places.**

1. You need to buy 💊 :
   ☐ drugstore    ☐ school

2. You need 🚂 :
   ☐ supermarket    ☐ bank

3. You want to drink ☕ :
   ☐ coffee shop    ☐ park

4. You need to buy 👗 :
   ☐ convenience store    ☐ mall

5. You need to buy 🍞 :
   ☐ school    ☐ convenience store

**Guess What!**
bike = bicycle
plane = airplane

**3 Classify the forms of transportation in the chart.**

Transportation
- Public: • _____ • _____ • _____ • _____
- Private: • _____ • _____ • _____

**4 Think Fast!** Count all the bikes, buses and motorcycles on the map.   2 min

**5** 🎧⁶ **Listen and circle the correct option.**

1. Alyssa is riding a **bike** / **motorcycle** to go to school.
2. Ben is getting on a **bus** / **train**.
3. Cathy is traveling on a **bus** / **plane**.
4. Dan is going to school by **subway** / **car**.

 29

# Grammar

**1** Read and follow the directions on the map.

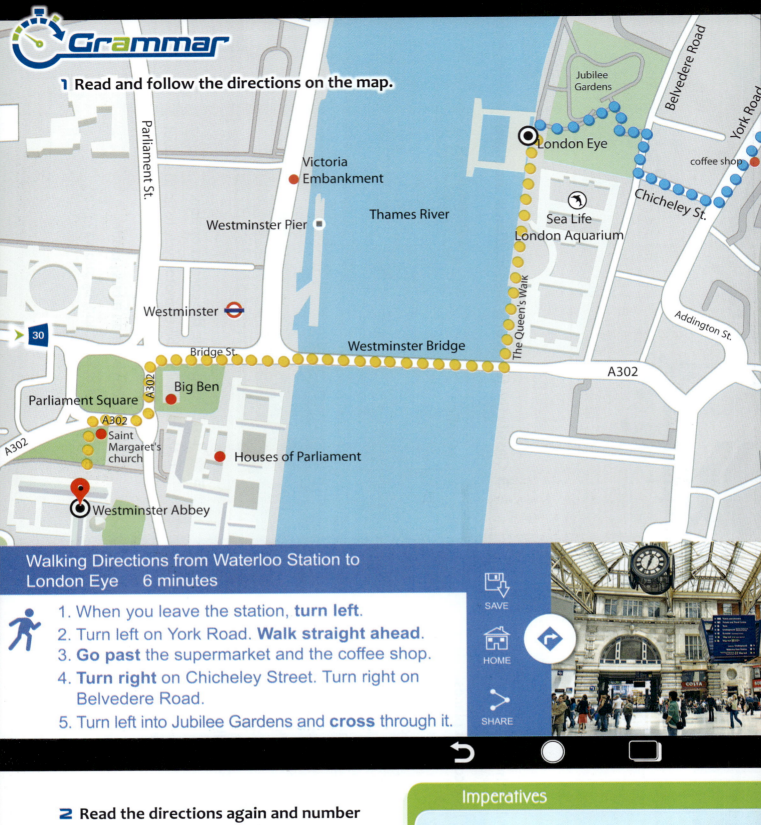

**Walking Directions from Waterloo Station to London Eye   6 minutes**

1. When you leave the station, **turn left**.
2. Turn left on York Road. **Walk straight ahead**.
3. **Go past** the supermarket and the coffee shop.
4. **Turn right** on Chicheley Street. Turn right on Belvedere Road.
5. Turn left into Jubilee Gardens and **cross** through it.

**2** Read the directions again and number the arrows.

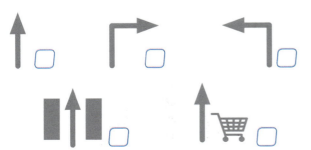

## Imperatives

Walk straight ahead... but don't go past the coffee shop.

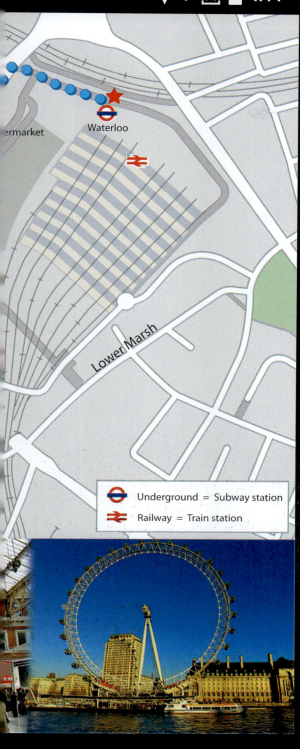

**3 Look at the signs. Correct the sentences.**

1
Don't stop here.
_____

2
Park your car here.
_____

3
Don't turn left.
_____

4
Drive over 50 km/h.
_____

5
Turn right.
_____

6
Ride your bike.
_____

**4 Think Fast!** In your notebook, write directions from the London Eye to Westminster Abbey.

**5** 🎧⁷ Listen to some tourists at Waterloo Station. Mark (✓) the correct options.

1. The girl thinks the London Eye is _____ tourist attraction in London.
   ☐ the best         ☐ the worst

2. Big Ben is _____ the London Eye.
   ☐ better than      ☐ farther than

3. Cars are _____ means of transportation for tourists in London.
   ☐ the fastest      ☐ the worst

### Comparatives and Superlatives – Irregular Forms

| Adjective | Comparative | Superlative |
|---|---|---|
| good | better than | the best |
| bad | worse than | the worst |
| far | farther than | the farthest |

 **Stop and Think!** In your opinion, what are the best and the worst places in your city?

# Listening & Reading

**1** 🎧⁸ **Listen to the directions and follow the route on the map. Write the places below.**

Destination 1: _____     Destination 2: _____

**2** Complete the instructions and write the destination. Start at the entrance of Green Park.

```
💬 📍                    ⏰ 🔋 📶 17:57
< DESTINATION
        We're ready. Let's go.
↑    _____ straight ahead on
     Orange Street to Oak Street.

←    _____ left on Oak Street.

↑    Walk straight ahead.
     Go past the coffee shop.

←    Turn left on Black Street.
     Your destination is on the left.

     Destination: _____
```

**3** Work with a partner. Give directions to a place on the map. Start at the X-Mall.

**Guess What!**
St. → Street
Ave. → Avenue

**Be Strategic!**
When you listen to directions, find the place where you are on a map.
Follow the route with your finger.

4 Look at the text below and mark (✓) its objective.
☐ to give information about signs   ☐ to advertise products   ☐ to give directions

5 Read the text again. Write the places in Chronopolis where the signs are located.
Sign 1: _____   Sign 2: _____   Sign 3: _____

| News | Shopping | Entertainment | What's On? | Videos | Maps | Sea |

# New Signs around Chronopolis

Text and photographs by Mary Sharp – What's On Special Reporter – Mar 11, 8:35 a.m.

Our magazine readers always tell us about funny and interesting things in the city. Let's look at some signs in public places. Check some of them out below (**click here** to see all the signs!). Can you guess where they are?

**An X-treme sign!**
This is a **huge billboard** outside some teenagers' favorite place in the city. What place does this sign advertise?

**Stop for the ducks!**
Believe it or not, this sign is in **downtown** Chronopolis… but where? **Pedestrians** and bike riders, **watch out for** Mother Duck and her ducklings!

**Keep calm and…**
*Keep calm* signs are very popular. This sign is stencil graffiti on the wall of a famous place in Chronopolis. It's located on Oak Street.

**Glossary**
**huge:** enormous
**billboard:** a big sign, outdoors
**downtown:** central area of a city
**pedestrians:** people that walk
**watch out for:** look out for something/ someone

6 Circle T (True) or F (False).

1. There are pictures from different cities.  T  F
2. You can see more pictures of signs on another web page.  T  F
3. The X-Mall sign is small.  T  F
4. It is difficult to find *Keep calm…* signs.  T  F
5. There are ducks in Chronopolis.  T  F

# Getting Around London:
## The Underground (or The Tube)

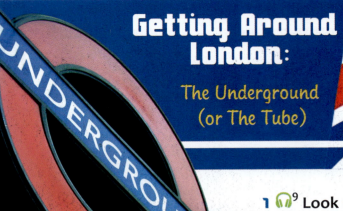

**1** 🎧⁹ **Look at the map. Listen and answer the questions.**
  1. What are the colors of the two **Underground** lines at Blackfriars Station?
  2. What is the name of the green line at Blackfriars Station?
  3. What colors are the Underground lines at Oxford Circus Station?

**2 Plan your trip to Oxford Circus.**
  Take the _____ line to _____.
  Change to the _____ line and travel to _____.

**3 Think Fast!** Plan a trip from Blackfriars Station to Hyde Park Corner.

**4 Read the timetable and answer in groups.**
  1. What line is this timetable for?
  2. What color is this line on the map?
  3. Is the timetable valid every day of the week?
  4. What time does the first train leave Heathrow Airport Terminal 5 (T5) on a weekday?

**Glossary**
**Underground:** the subway in the UK, especially London

## PICCADILLY LINE
### FROM MONDAYS TO SATURDAYS

| | First trains | | | PX | | Last trains | | | |
|---|---|---|---|---|---|---|---|---|---|
| | | | | 0523 | ... | ... | 2342 | 2400 | 0018 |
| Heathrow T5 | ... | ... | 0523 | ... | 0005 | 0009 | 0027 | 0045 | 0112 |
| Acton Town | 0526 | 0536 | 0551 | 0557 | 0013 | 0017 | 0036 | ... | ... |
| Hammersmith | 0534 | 0544 | 0559 | 0605 | 0018 | 0022 | ... | ... | ... |
| Earl's Court | 0539 | 0549 | 0604 | 0610 | 0029 | 0034 | ... | ... | ... |
| Piccadilly Circus | 0550 | 0600 | 0615 | 0621 | | | | | |

**PX** On Saturdays only.
For additional trains between Heathrow and Acton Town see the Train Times posters at the stations.

**Key to lines and symbols**
- Bakerloo
- Central
- Circle
- District
- East London
- Hammersmith & City
- Jubilee
- Metropolitan
- Northern
- Piccadilly
- Victoria

 **Stop and Think**! How can you be respectful of people on public transportation?

**1** Work in pairs. Complete the table about the means of transportation in your city.

🛢 uses fossil fuel
🍃 eco-friendly

| Means of Transportation: | In My Town? | Ecological Impact | Rating |
|---|---|---|---|
| 🚗 | too many! | 🛢 🍃 | ★☆☆☆☆ |
| ✈️ | | 🛢 🍃 | ☆☆☆☆☆ |
| 🚲 | | 🛢 🍃 | ☆☆☆☆☆ |
| 🚕 | | 🛢 🍃 | ☆☆☆☆☆ |
| 🚆 | | 🛢 🍃 | ☆☆☆☆☆ |
| 🚌 | | 🛢 🍃 | ☆☆☆☆☆ |
| 🚂 | | 🛢 🍃 | ☆☆☆☆☆ |
| 🏍 | | 🛢 🍃 | ☆☆☆☆☆ |
| Other: | | 🛢 🍃 | ☆☆☆☆☆ |

**2** Work with a partner to answer the questions.

1. Are people happy with the means of transportation in your city?
2. Are there efficient, eco-friendly means of transportation in your city?

**3** Brainstorm a new, eco-friendly means of transportation.

| Means of Transportation | Name and Logo | Type of Renewable Fuel | Route |
|---|---|---|---|
| | | | |

**4** Create a poster to present your proposal.

**Tips**
1. Take some time to practice your presentation.
2. Try not to read from a paper while speaking. You can improvise if necessary.

**Glossary**
**fossil fuel:** gasoline, natural gas, coal
**eco-friendly:** doesn't use fuel or uses renewable fuel

**5 Present your proposal to your classmates.**

Speak clearly. Take turns with your partner.

Some useful expressions:

- Good morning / afternoon.
- Our proposal for a new means of transportation in _____ is a
  city
  _____.
  means of transportation
- We call it "_____" and this is its logo.
  name
- It runs on _____.
  type of renewable fuel
- It goes from _____ to _____.
  place in the city        place in the city

# Review

**1** Number the pictures. What place does each picture suggest?

1. bank
2. convenience store
3. coffee shop
4. drugstore
5. mall
6. park
7. school
8. supermarket

**2** Look and label.

3 **Draw signs for the instructions.**

| | | | |
|---|---|---|---|
| 1. Turn left. | 2. Don't walk here. | 3. Stop. | 4. Don't turn right. |

4 **Complete the chart.**

| Irregular Comparative and Superlative Forms | | |
|---|---|---|
| | Comparative | Superlative |
| 👍 good | | |
| 👎 bad | | |
| ☞ far | | |

5 **Write sentences using the comparative form.**

1. Willow Park / far from downtown / Green Park

   _____

2. CSB Drugstore / good / Willow Drugstore

   _____

3. Planet Coffee Shop / bad / Awesome Coffee Shop

   _____

4. Emma's middle school / far from her house / her primary school

   _____

6 **In your notebook, write four sentences using the superlative form. Use the information in the chart.**

| The Best and the Worst in Timeville | | |
|---|---|---|
| | ★ | ★★★★★ |
| coffee shop | Roasted | Carla's Coffee |
| supermarket | T-Mart | Food Boutique |

# Just for Fun

**1** Find the places in the word search (→, ↓ or ↘). Mark (X) the missing word.

- ☐ bank
- ☐ coffee shop
- ☐ drugstore
- ☐ mall
- ☐ park
- ☐ school
- ☐ supermarket

```
L Z D G L O B W L G C T
C X E F G Q A S T H D A
Z S V J Z Q U M P A R K
Y R A L G E F Z B H U F
G F K O Q I M P A B G F
S J W C A M G U N F S M
S U P E R M A R K E T V
E I N S I S G L F E O H
A T T S C H O O L K R G
I N U W R E O B T H E Y
```

**2** Write the forms of transportation that you can't see!

bike   bus   car   taxi

**1**

_____

**2**

_____

**3**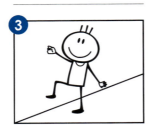

_____

**4**

_____

**3** Unscramble the words. Use the numbered letters to find the secret direction.

1. Turn TIRHG.   
   8 9 10 6

2. Turn FLET.  
   3 12

3. COSRS the park.  
   7 5

4. LAWK past the school.  
   1 2 4

5. NOD'T cross the street.  
   13 11

1 2 3 4   5 6 7 2 8 9 10 11   2 10 12 2 13

**4** Solve the spiral puzzle.

1. comparative form of *far*
2. superlative form of *good*
3. comparative form of *bad*
4. superlative form of *far*
5. comparative form of *good*
6. superlative form of *bad*

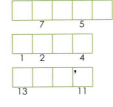

| Start → | ¹f | | | | | |
|---|---|---|---|---|---|---|
| | | | | 5 | | |
| | | | → Finish | | | ²b |
| | | | 6 | | | |
| ⁴ | | | | ³ | | |

# Vocabulary

**1** Look at the picture and describe the girl.

**2** 🎧¹⁰ Listen and mark (✓) the correct option.

Description 1 ☐    Description 2 ☐    Description 3 ☐

> **Guess What!**
> The word *avatar* was first used for the representation of a player in a video game in 1985!

**3 Complete the descriptions of the avatars.**

1. K-Man is _____ and chubby. He has _____ black hair and dark eyes.
2. MsSunshine is medium height and _____. She has long _____ hair and gray _____.

① K-Man

② MsSunshine

③ SoccerJim

④ MrTie

43

**2 min**

**4 Think Fast! Describe the other two avatars.**

**5 Complete the descriptions using the avatar names.**

① Ms. Marr is a math teacher. She's **kind:** she always helps her students. Her avatar is _____.

② Mr. Bowers is **shy.** He doesn't like to talk to people. But his avatar isn't shy! It's _____.

③ Ken isn't **serious.** He tells jokes all the time: he's **funny!** His avatar is _____.

④ James likes sports and he's **intelligent:** he always gets good grades in school. His avatar is _____.

**6 🎧 11 Listen and number.**

1. Jesse ☐ rude
2. Will ☐ shy
3. Olivia ☐ intelligent
4. Luke ☐ funny

**Stop and Think!** Describe a friend.

**Guess What!**
Some adjectives have opposites:

kind ≠ rude

shy ≠ outgoing

funny ≠ serious

## Grammar

**1** Read and circle the correct option.

> Do you have a good friend?
> Does your friend really like you?
> Are you a good or a bad friend?

A good friend **helps** / **doesn't help** you.

Good friends **argue** / **don't argue** a lot.

A good friend **tells** / **doesn't tell** your secrets to other people.

A good friend **feels** / **doesn't feel** happy for you.

A good friend **respects** / **doesn't respect** your differences.

Good friends **get** / **don't get jealous**.

**2** Write sentences in affirmative (✓) or negative (✗).

1. Jack and Connor / have any secrets / ✗

   _____

2. Emily / agree with Mia / (✓)

   _____

3. Carlos / like Saul's friends / ✗

   _____

4. Mason and Sue / help each other solve problems / (✓)

   _____

# TOP TEENS MAGAZINE

**3 Look and circle the correct options.**

Ethan and his friend **are** / **is** watching a horror movie.

This is me! I **'m** / **'re** skateboarding.

Today, Abby **are** / **is** walking to school. Her friends **are** / **is** walking with her.

Here Aidan and his cousins **am** / **are** playing video games.

**4 Read and number.**

1. Is Ethan watching a horror movie?
2. Are you playing volleyball?
3. Is Abby walking to the mall?
4. Are they playing a racing game?

☐ Yes, they are.
☐ No, she isn't. She's walking to school.
☐ Yes, he is.
☐ No, I'm not. I'm skateboarding.

### Simple vs. Continuous

We use **present simple** to talk about a general truth.
We use **present continuous** for an action at the moment of speaking.

**5 Think Fast!** Mime activities for classmates to guess.

### Glossary
**argue:** to disagree or fight with words

**jealous:** to feel that someone has something that is yours and they shouldn't have it

## Listening & Writing

## Summer Camp in Vancouver

Visit Vancouver and make new friends on a two-week trip!

Go camping, play sports, _____, swim, _____ and explore!

Scholarships are available. Submit your application before April 15.

For information, contact school counselor Mr. Dale.

THREE OWLS MIDDLE SCHOOL

## Canada Summer Program

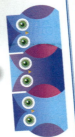
THREE OWLS MIDDLE SCHOOL

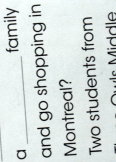

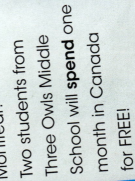

Learn French and have fun in Quebec for one month! Do you want to learn a _____, live with _____ family and go shopping in Montreal? Two students from Three Owls Middle School will **spend** one month in Canada for FREE!

**Fill out** the form at the school office before March _____. **Interviews** with school counselor Mr. Dale are March 25 - 29.

# Be Strategic!

A speaker's tone of voice can express what she is feeling. For example, a speaker's tone can express a strong opinion, surprise or uncertainty.

## Glossary

**spend (time):** pass time in a place
**fill out:** complete information in a form
**interview:** a meeting to obtain information, normally between two people
**without:** the opposite of with
**cool:** very good

**1** 🎧 12 **Listen and identify the poster.**

**2 Complete the information on the poster.**

### Guess What!

We use *why* and *because* to ask and answer about reasons.

*Why do you like English?*
*Because it's a beautiful language.*

**4 Fill out the form.**

## Summer Camp in Vancouver

THREE OWLS MIDDLE SCHOOL

Name: _____
Age: _____
Grade: _____

1. Why do you want to participate in the summer camp?
Because _____

2. Why do you want to visit Canada?
_____

3. What sports do you like?
_____

4. Can you travel **without** your parents?
_____

5. What makes you a good friend?
_____

**3** 🎧 13 **Listen and mark (✓) the correct answers.**

1. Why does Riley want to participate in the summer program?
Because...
☐ she likes to study French.
☐ she wants to travel **without** her family.
☐ she wants to learn about Canadian culture.

2. Why does Chloe want to participate in the summer program?
Because...
☐ she likes to study French.
☐ she wants to have fun in Montreal.
☐ she thinks Canada is a **cool** country.

 **Stop and Think!** What can you learn by studying in another country?

47

# Culture: Cosplay

## 1 Read the encyclopedia entry. Then circle T (True) or F (False).

1. The word *cosplay* is the combination of three other words.   T   F
2. Cosplayers dress as anime, manga and video game characters.   T   F
3. There are no special events and meetings for cosplayers.   T   F
4. The Japanese word for business cards is *meishi*.   T   F

**Cosplay** – the practice of **dressing up** as a character—usually from *manga*, *anime* or video games. Cosplay has its origins in Japan, where it is pronounced *cosupure* (コスモード).

The word *cosplay* comes from the words *costume* and *play*. Sometimes *cosplayers* (the people who participate in this activity) also speak and walk like their characters. Cosplayers plan and create their costumes carefully. Most cosplayers in Japan have their own *meishi*, or business cards. Cosplayers exchange cards at meetings and events.

 **2 Think Fast!** Look and identify: an anime illustration, a *meishi* card and a picture of cosplay from fantasy, history and video games.

Midori

**3** 🎧¹⁴ **Listen and answer. Why does Midori like cosplay?**
1. Because she loves _____.
2. Because she can become _____.
3. Because she can make _____.

**4** **Answer *Yes, she does* or *No, she doesn't*.**
1. Does Midori have a favorite manga character? _____
2. Does she go to cosplay conventions in the United States? _____
3. Does she put on her costume quickly? _____
4. Does she feel shy when she dresses up? _____

**Guess What!**
In stores, cosplay costumes can cost up to $300. That does not include shoes, a wig, a hat and other accessories!

**Stop and Think!** Do you need to be really good at a hobby to enjoy it?

Japan

**Glossary**
**dress up:** wear special clothes, like costumes, for fun

wig         hat

**1** Organize the words from the cloud in the chart.

FUNNY  SERIOUS  KIND  RUDE  INTELLIGENT  SHY  OUTGOING

| Characteristics |||
|---|---|---|
| Positive | Neutral | Negative |
|  |  |  |

 **Stop and Think!** How do people feel when you use negative words to describe them?

**2** Look and number the thought bubbles.

☐ I'm very shy.

☐ My friends are talking about me.

☐ I'm not intelligent.

☐ I'm chubby.

3 **Make a self-care kit.**

**Step 1:**
Get a box to store the items in your kit. You can also use a zipper storage bag.

**Step 2:**
Write a list of things that make you feel better in difficult times.

**Step 3:**
Pick up items related to your list that could be stored in the box / bag.

**Step 4:**
Keep the box in an accessible place, so that you can often see it.

**Step 5:**
Use one or more items from your box whenever you need to feel better!

**Tips!**
You can include an item from the time you were a child—choose something that brings happy memories, for example, a stuffed animal.
Add or change the items in your self-care kit whenever you want.

# Review

**1 Classify the words.**

black   blond   brown   chubby   intelligent   long
outgoing   rude   short   shy   tall   thin

| Physical Description | | Personality Traits |
|---|---|---|
| **Hair** | **Body** | |
| | | |

**2 Look and complete the descriptions.**

Jake, Grace, Zoe, Ava and Alan are very good friends.

1. Jake is _____ and thin. He has very short _____ hair.
2. Grace is short and medium _____. She has _____ brown hair.
3. Zoe is _____ height. She has _____ brown hair.
4. Ava has long _____ hair. She is _____ and thin.
5. Alan is tall and _____. He has _____ straight blond hair.

**3 Complete the sentences using the verb in the affirmative or negative form.**

1. Kylie is a good friend. She _____ (*respect*) her friends' ideas.

2. Sean and Elijah are good friends. They _____ (*criticize*) each other's opinions.

3. I think I'm a good friend. I _____ (*tell*) my friends' secrets to other people.

4. Alex is a good friend. He _____ (*listen*) to his friends.

**4 Look at the pictures and write sentences.**

have a picnic    run    play soccer    read a book

1. They are _____

2. She _____

3. _____

4. _____

**5 Write the complete questions.**

1. you / play video games / ? _____

   No, I'm not. I'm watching TV.

2. Josh / walk to school / ? _____

   Yes, he is.

3. Ella / play soccer / ? _____

   No, she isn't. She's playing baseball.

4. Tyler and Noah / skateboard / ? _____

   Yes, they are.

# Just for Fun

**1** Use opposites to solve the puzzle.

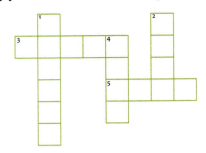

**Down**
1. thin
2. chubby
4. short (height)

**Across**
3. tall
5. short (hair)

**2** Write the celebrities' names.

**Hugh Jackman**      **Katy Perry**      **Emma Watson**      **Jim Parsons**

1. _____ doesn't have a beard or a mustache. He doesn't play Wolverine in the X-Men movies.
2. _____ doesn't have short hair and brown eyes. She's not from the UK.
3. _____ doesn't have blue eyes. He doesn't play a very intelligent scientist in a TV series.
4. _____ doesn't have dark hair and green eyes. She's not a singer.

**3** Circle four positive words in the word snake.

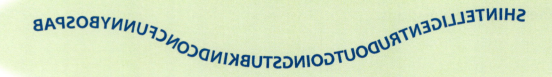

Vertumnus, by Giuseppe Arcimboldo (1591)

# What do we eat?

4

# Vocabulary

**1** Write the food items in the correct category.

oranges

milk

onions

beans

rice

water

**2** 🎧¹⁵ **Listen and check.**

**3** Listen again and complete the sentences.

1. Isabella likes _____, _____ and _____.
2. She doesn't like _____, _____ or _____.

**OPTIONS FOR**

**FRUIT**
bananas
apples

**VEGETABLES**
carrots
broccoli

**Guess What!**
People usually have three main **meals** during the day: **breakfast**, **lunch** and **dinner**.

After lunch or dinner, people can have a **dessert**.

# A PERFECT PLATE

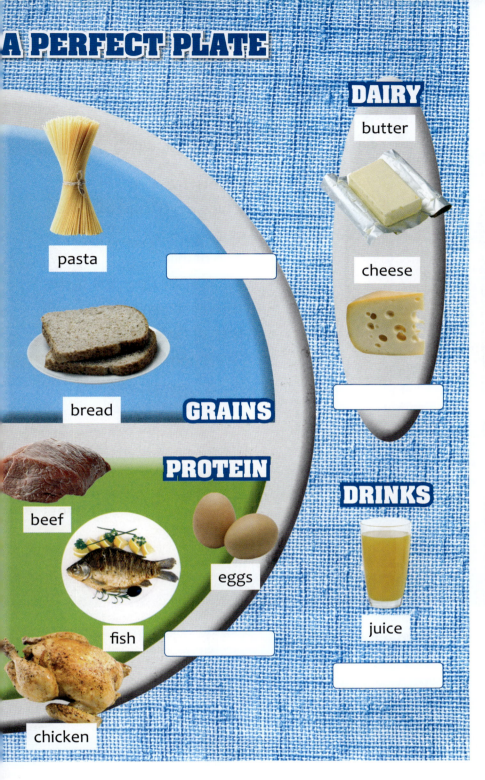

DAIRY
butter
cheese

GRAINS
pasta
bread

PROTEIN
beef
fish
eggs
chicken

DRINKS
juice

**4** 🎧 **16** Listen and mark (✓) what they eat and drink.

|  |  | Lucas | Abby |
|---|---|---|---|
| Food | 🍎 |  |  |
|  | 🫘 |  |  |
|  | 🍗 |  |  |
|  | 🐟 |  |  |
|  | 🥕 |  |  |
|  | 🍚 |  |  |
|  | 🍅 |  |  |
| Drinks | 🧃 |  |  |
|  | 🥛 |  |  |

 **5 Think Fast!** Say three food items you like and two you don't like.

 **Stop and Think!** Why do we eat and drink things we don't like?

**6** Complete the table with your ideas.

| I like this and I eat/drink it! | I don't like this but I eat/drink it! | I don't like this and I don't eat/drink it! |
|---|---|---|
|  |  |  |

# Grammar

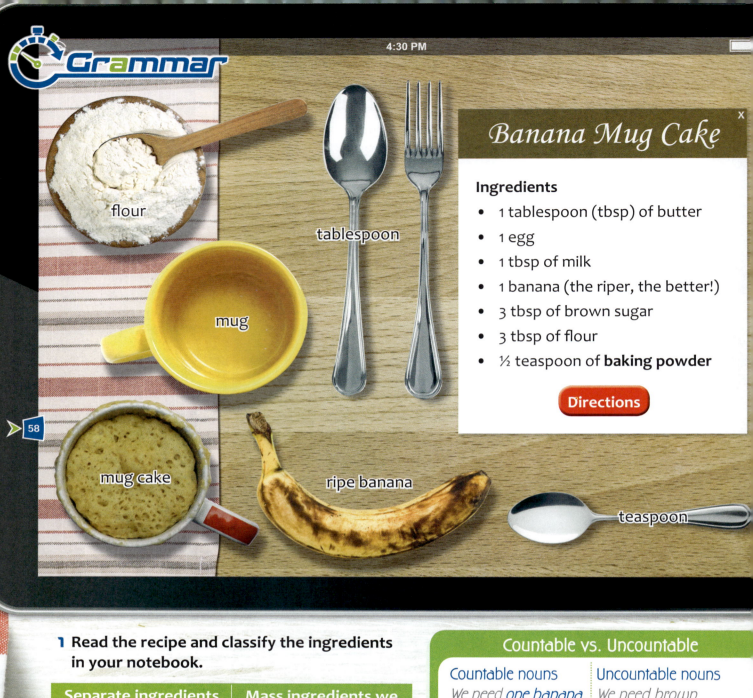

**Banana Mug Cake**

**Ingredients**
- 1 tablespoon (tbsp) of butter
- 1 egg
- 1 tbsp of milk
- 1 banana (the riper, the better!)
- 3 tbsp of brown sugar
- 3 tbsp of flour
- ½ teaspoon of **baking powder**

Directions

**1** Read the recipe and classify the ingredients in your notebook.

| Separate ingredients we can count (Countable nouns) | Mass ingredients we need to measure (Uncountable nouns) |
|---|---|
| | |

### Countable vs. Uncountable

**Countable nouns**
We need **one banana**.

**Uncountable nouns**
We need brown **sugar**, too.

**2** Look again at Activity 1, page 56. Add four items to the table in your notebook.

**3** Mark the sentence + (affirmative), – (negative) or ? (a question).
1. ☐ We don't have **any** butter to make **a** mug cake.
2. ☐ Are there **any** onions?
3. ☐ Please buy **some** eggs and **some** milk.
4. ☐ Do you have **any** flour?
5. ☐ There are **some** oranges and **an** apple on the table.
6. ☐ There aren't **any** tomatoes in the fridge.

**G**lossary
**baking powder:** this makes the dough rise in cakes

**4 Complete the information.**

a an any some

1. (+) We have _____ tomatoes.
2. (–) We don't have _____ onions.
3. (?) Are there _____ carrots?
4. (+) There is _____ carrot on the table.
5. (–) We don't have _____ milk.
6. (+) There is _____ spaghetti.
7. (+) There is _____ apple here.

**5 Complete the notes.**

1. To make a fruit salad, I need
   two _____,
   a green _____,
   an _____
   and some _____.

apple   bananas
orange   yogurt

2. For Bolognese sauce, I need a 🥄
   of butter, an _____,
   six ripe _____,
   some _____, two 🥛 of
   _____ and two carrots.

beef   water
onion   tomatoes

3. To make a Special Apple Pie,
   I need five big _____,
   a 🥛 of _____ juice,
   an _____,
   one 🥄 of _____
   and some flour.

apples   baking soda
egg   flour
orange

**6 🎧¹⁷ Listen and mark
✓ (There is/are some) or
✗ (There isn't/aren't any).**

eggs ☐
orange juice ☐
flour ☐
apples ☐
baking soda ☐

**Guess What!**
May 13 is National
Apple Pie Day in the
United States!

# Reading & Speaking

**1** **Look at the phone screens and circle T (True) or F (False).**

1. The texts are about restaurants.     T    F
2. All the restaurants are similar.     T    F
3. The texts have different people's opinions.     T    F

**Be Strategic!**
To improve your comprehension, read the text quickly to identify the main ideas. Then read it again slowly.

**2** **Read the texts more carefully. Mark (✓) all the correct options.**

|  | The Veggie Place | Sam's Diner | Pampered Pizza | Antonella's |
|---|---|---|---|---|
| 1. There isn't any beef or chicken on the menu. | | | | |
| 2. There aren't any tables to eat here. | | | | |
| 3. There are Italian dishes on the menu. | | | | |
| 4. There are reduced prices for people who study. | | | | |
| 5. The servers are rude to young people. | | | | |

**3** 🎧¹⁸ **Listen and number the speakers.**

Brianna2003 ☐   BeautifulBelle ☐
AustinPeace ☐   GourmetSean04 ☐

**4 Categorize the words in a chart in your notebook: *positive* (+), *negative* (−) and *both* (+ −).**

**5 Ask and answer with a classmate.**

How do you like...?

I like it a lot. / I love it!
I don't like it at all. / I hate it.

Why?

The options on the menu...
The food is...
The prices are...
The servers are...

| Symbols | | | |
|---|---|---|---|
| okay | 😐 | good | 🙂 |
| great | 😀 | delicious | 😋 |
| awful | 😠 | bad | 🙁 |
| gross | 🤢 | awesome | 😎 |
| cheap | $ | expensive | $$$ |

**Glossary**

**takeout:** food you take home

**healthy:** good for your body (opposite: unhealthy)

**server:** a person that takes food to your table at a restaurant

## La Tomatina

La Tomatina is a famous festival that occurs in the small city of Bunol, Spain, in the month of August. Every year, around 20,000 participants throw **squashed** tomatoes at each other in a dirty **food fight**. In preparation of the day, there are events with music, dancing, food and **fireworks**.

On the day of the event, **trucks** bring the tomatoes to the *Plaza del Pueblo*. When participants hear a loud sound, the fight begins! At 11 o'clock, participants start to throw tomatoes at everyone—friends and strangers—in the biggest food fight in the world! One hour later, at 12 o'clock, there is another loud sound and La Tomatina is over. Now it's time to get cleaned up!

### La Tomatina's numbers!

| 20,000 | 1945 | 150,000 | €10 |
|---|---|---|---|
| the number of participants every year | the year of the first La Tomatina festival | the number of tomatoes used in the food fight | the price of a ticket for La Tomatina |

---

**1 Read the first paragraph and complete the sentences.**

1. La Tomatina happens in the Spanish city of _____.
2. The festival is always in the month of _____.
3. During the food fight, people throw _____.

**2 Read the rest of the article and underline the answers in the article.**

1. How many people participate in *La Tomatina*?
2. How long do participants throw tomatoes?
3. When was the first *Tomatina* held?

**3** 🎧¹⁹ **Listen and match. What are the visitors' opinions?**

1. Mia          La Tomatina can be a dangerous activity.
2. Connor       It's fun!
3. Chloe        It's a waste of good food.

**4** 🎧¹⁹ **Listen again and mark (✓) the ideas you hear.**

1. ☐ You can take good pictures with a cell phone.
2. ☐ People eat a lot of tomato soup at the festival.
3. ☐ You can fall and hurt your body.
4. ☐ You need to wear old clothes and sneakers.

**Stop and Think!** Is it OK to waste large amounts of food in festivals such as *La Tomatina*?

### Glossary

**squashed:** to press into a mass

**food fight:** an unusual activity where people throw food at each other for fun

**fireworks:**

**truck:** a vehicle used for moving heavy objects

63

# Project

**1** Label the food and drink items in the tables. Use the words provided.

apple pie   baked potato   chocolate cream cookies
orange juice   popcorn   ice cream

## Table A

| whole wheat cookies | homemade _____ | _____ apples |
|---|---|---|
| _____ | popsicle | _____ |

## Table B

| _____ | microwave popcorn | _____ |
|---|---|---|
| orange soda | _____ | French fries |

**2** Complete the Venn diagram. How are Table A and Table B similar and different?

Table A        Table B

**Guess What!** In the US, 22 million students receive free or reduced price lunches.

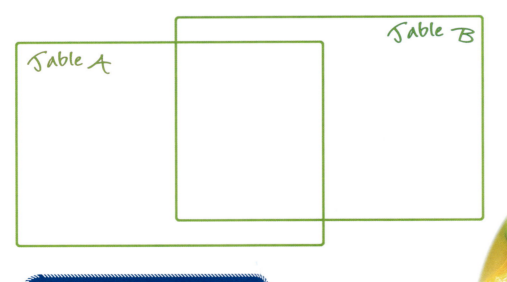

# Little Creek Middle School Cafeteria

### Sandwiches
All sandwiches served with white bread
| | |
|---|---|
| Double cheeseburger | $ 6.50 |
| Hot dog | $ 4.25 |
| Ham and cheese | $ 3.00 |

### Salads
| | |
|---|---|
| Lettuce and tomato | $ 6.00 |

### Side orders
| | |
|---|---|
| French fries | $ 2.50 |
| Onion rings | $ 2.00 |

### Desserts
| | |
|---|---|
| Ice cream | $ 1.50 |
| Chocolate chip cookies | $ 1.75 |

### Beverages
| | |
|---|---|
| Soda | $ 0.75 |

**3** Read the menu and circle the healthy options.

**4** Work with a partner. Write a healthy menu.
1. Analyze the food and drink items on the menu. How can they be healthier?
2. List healthy options for the sections of the menu. Include the categories below.
3. Copy your new menu on a sheet of paper. Make your menu attractive for the customers!
4. Share your menu with your classmates. Which menu is the healthiest / the most attractive?

## Menu

Sandwiches

Side Orders

Beverages

Salads

Desserts

# Review

**1 Unscramble the words.**

1. F E B E  _____
2. L I K M  _____
3. E C E S E H  _____
4. I H S F  _____
5. T U T E R B  _____
6. T A S P A  _____

**2 Complete the crossword.**

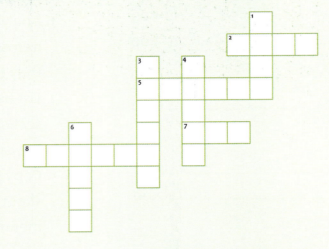

**Down**

1. This grain is very popular in China and Japan.
3. You need this vegetable to make Bolognese sauce.
4. The healthiest drink.
6. Some people have this for breakfast, with butter.

**Across**

2. Salmon and tuna are popular kinds of this food.
5. The most popular fruit to make juice.
7. You can eat this fried, scrambled or in an omelet.
8. People say this vegetable is good for the eyes.

**3 Organize the items from Activities 1 and 2. Then add two other items to each column.**

| Things I like to eat for breakfast: | Things I like to eat for lunch: | Things I like to eat for dinner: |
|---|---|---|
|  |  |  |

4 **Look at the underlined words. Write C (countable) or U (uncountable).**
1. Do you like pineapple juice?
2. We need three bananas to make the pie.
3. I always have fried chicken for lunch.
4. We need two apples for the fruit salad.
5. Ann doesn't eat beef. She's a vegetarian.
6. My brother doesn't like broccoli.

5 **Circle the correct option.**
1. They need to buy **some** / **any** tomatoes for the sauce.
2. Do you have **some** / **any** milk?
3. Luke doesn't like **some** / **any** butter on his bread.
4. Is there **some** / **any** ice cream in the fridge?
5. Ella eats **some** / **any** fish every week.
6. They don't have **some** / **any** lettuce for the salad.

6 **Look and write the missing ingredient.**

Ingredients
1/2 cup olive oil
1 medium onion
2 carrots
½ kilo ground beef
½ kilo _____
¼ cup cheese
salt and pepper
garlic and thyme
½ kilo pasta

7 **Mark (✓) the correct dish.**

☐ Rustic pizza    ☐ Spaghetti bolognese    ☐ Vegetable soup

# Just for Fun

**1** Use the letters in the box to write ten food words.

| A | B | C | E |
|---|---|---|---|
| G | I | L | N |
| O | P | R | S |
| T | U | W | Y |

_____  _____

_____  _____

_____  _____

_____  _____

_____  _____

**2** Find food items → ↓ and draw them in the boxes.

```
U H I M G B U T T E R B
B S U I C A O T H W P F
R R I C E G G S F H X O
M C Z B B Z Y T T I N B
V H W R P M O A F C U E
Y E O E X I G Z R K H A
I E J A M L U H W E C N
L S Y D K K R T D N W S
J E R N U N T B E E F C
```

I like to eat:

I don't like to eat:

**3** Play tic-tac-toe with a classmate. Create sentences with the words.

| a | glass | a little |
|---|---|---|
| cup | Choose the word | any |
| some | an | table-spoon |

**4** Read and circle *T* (True) or *F* (False).

1. The word *potato* comes from the Portuguese word *batata*.  T  F
2. There is a field of science dedicated to fruit. It is called *pomology*.  T  F
3. An average chicken lays 100 eggs a year.  T  F
4. The first breakfast cereal was invented in the 19th century.  T  F

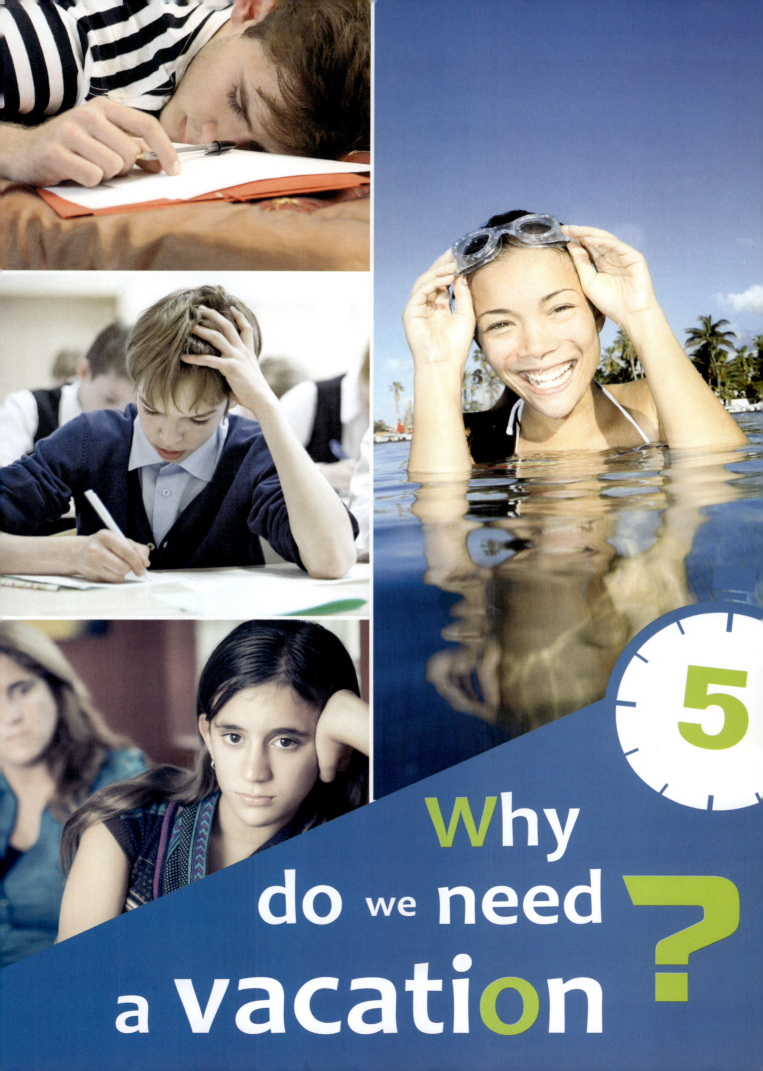

# Vocabulary

**1** 🎧 [20] Label the pictures. Then listen and check.

- amusement park
- aquarium
- art museum
- beach
- historic center
- mountains
- street market
- zoo

## The Ultimate Teen Travel Guide
### The Beach or the Mountains?

### Top Attractions in Triple Peaks

Average temperature: 8° C  Average hotel price: $$$
Average restaurant price: $$

①   ②

③   ④

### Top Attractions in Bongo Beach

Average temperature: 28° C  Average hotel price: $$$$
Average restaurant price: $$$

①   ②

③   ④

**2** Think Fast! List the attractions you can a) probably find in Hawaii, and b) visit in your town or city. (3 min)

**Glossary**
**average:** a typical level

## Bongo Beach – Practical Information

- **Mango Beach** in Bongo is **great** ★★★! It's the best beach in the city. Good for surfing, playing and relaxing and having **fun** ★★★. You can take **beautiful** selfies ★★★ with the ocean.

- The **restaurants on Bongo Beach** are good ★★☆. But the food at the Hamburger Place is **terrible** ☆☆☆!

- The **Bongo Art Museum** is a **boring** place ★☆☆. The art works aren't interesting.

- The **Downtown Street Market** is very **noisy** ★☆☆. There is music everywhere; you can't have a conversation. And it's always **crowded** ★☆☆—there are hundreds of people.

- The **Bongo Aquarium** is **great** ★★★! You need 3 hours to see it all!

 **3 Think Fast!** Look at the information and identify the best attractions of Bongo Beach.

**Guess What!** *Praia do Cassino*, in the south of Brazil, is the longest beach in the world. It is 254 km long!

 71

**4** Read the information. Then read and match.

1. great beaches
2. a fun activity
3. beautiful pictures
4. terrible food
5. a boring museum
6. a noisy restaurant
7. a crowded place

☐ very bad, horrible
☐ attractive photos
☐ very good, excellent for swimming
☐ not interesting to visit
☐ full of sounds, not quiet
☐ an exciting thing to do
☐ with many people

 **Stop and Think!** What do you prefer for a vacation, the beach or the mountains? Why?

## 3 Circle the correct verbs.

1. In the story, Ann and Dan **was** / **were** at Ann's house.
2. Dan **was** / **wasn't** in the pictures with Ann.
3. Ann's parents **was** / **were** in one of the pictures.
4. They **were** / **weren't** in Paris, France.
5. Ann **was** / **wasn't** angry after the water ride.
6. Ann and her parents **were** / **weren't** at an amusement park in Florida.

## 4 Match the questions to the answers.

1. In one of the pictures, was Ann on a camel? ___ No, he wasn't. He was laughing.
2. Was Ann in a picture with her parents? ___ Yes, they were.
3. Where was Ann in picture number 5? ___ No, she wasn't.
4. Were Ann and her parents at an amusement park? ___ Yes, she was, but not in Egypt.
5. Was Dan angry with Ann at the end of the story? ___ She was in Florida.

**5 Think Fast!** In your notebook, write two more questions about the comic using *was* and *were*.

Present → Past

am, is → was (neg. wasn't)
are → were (neg. weren't)

73

Baby kangaroos are called "joeys."

**Be Strategic!**
Predict the information you expect to hear. Do you expect personal names, countries, numbers or other words?

**2** 🎧²² Listen to Isabella's presentation and confirm your answers.

**3** 🎧²² Read the sentences and predict the words. Then listen and complete the sentences.

| Egypt | 1. The country was very _____. |
| --- | --- |
| | 2. The street markets were _____. |
| China | 3. Places were _____. |
| | 4. Eating insects was _____. |
| Australia | 5. Bondi Beach in Sydney was _____. |
| | 6. The girls with the kangaroos are Isabella's _____. |

**4** Circle the correct words.
1. Scrapbooks present **personal** / **academic** information.
2. People generally use scrapbooks to register **special moments** / **important notes**.
3. People usually include lots of **text** / **pictures** in their scrapbooks.

**5** Now write a page for a vacation scrapbook—print or digital. Follow the steps below.
1. Think of a vacation—real or imaginary.
2. Collect pictures to include in your scrapbook.
3. Add boxes with text to describe individual images.

75

# Culture

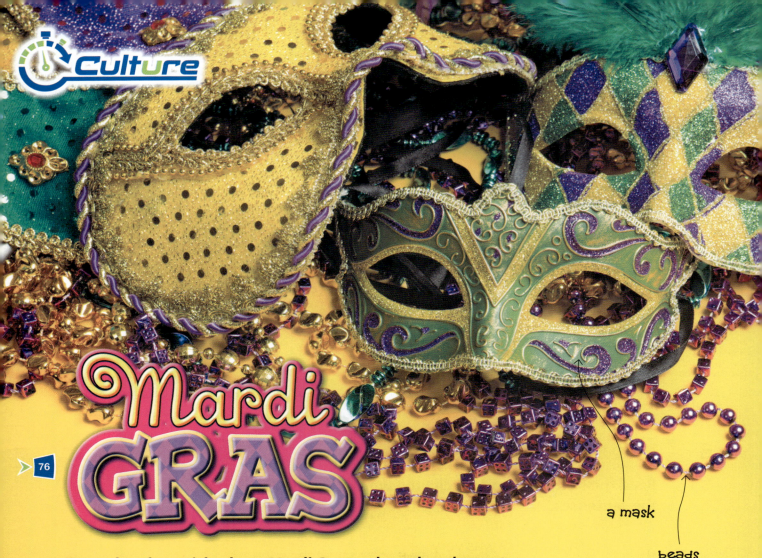

a mask
beads

# Mardi Gras

**1** Read at the article about Mardi Gras and number the parts.

☐ What to see ☐ Introduction ☐ Details about food

## CELEBRATING CARNIVAL IN THE UNITED STATES

1. Mardi Gras is the celebration of Carnival in New Orleans. The first American Mardi Gras was organized by French colonizers around 1700.

2. Nowadays, over a million people enjoy Mardi Gras in New Orleans. They watch **parades** on the streets, with large and colorful **floats**. The most important parade includes the king of Carnival, called "Rex," and the queen. Bands play jazz music during the parades.

3. The traditional food of Mardi Gras is the King cake—a cake with a small plastic baby inside. People eat the cake with friends and family. According to the tradition, the person who finds the doll in the cake will be lucky during the year.

**Guess What!**
The expression *Mardi Gras* ("Fat Tuesday") comes from French. Tuesday is the last day of the Carnival celebrations.

**Glossary**
**parade:** a public celebration that includes marching in the street or watching decorated vehicles called **floats**

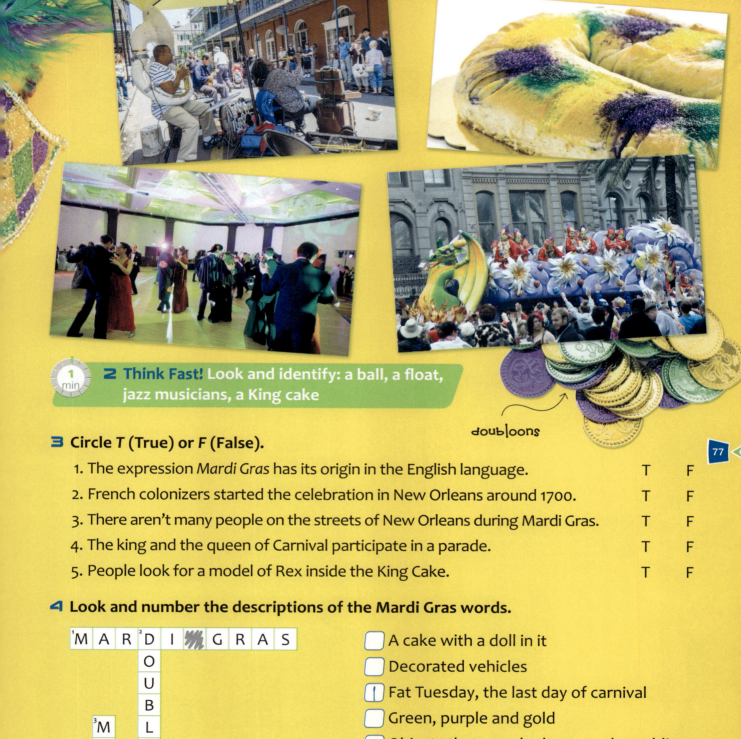

**2 Think Fast!** Look and identify: a ball, a float, jazz musicians, a King cake

doubloons

**3 Circle T (True) or F (False).**

1. The expression *Mardi Gras* has its origin in the English language.   T   F
2. French colonizers started the celebration in New Orleans around 1700.   T   F
3. There aren't many people on the streets of New Orleans during Mardi Gras.   T   F
4. The king and the queen of Carnival participate in a parade.   T   F
5. People look for a model of Rex inside the King Cake.   T   F

**4 Look and number the descriptions of the Mardi Gras words.**

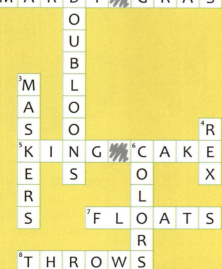

- ☐ A cake with a doll in it
- ☐ Decorated vehicles
- ☑ Fat Tuesday, the last day of carnival
- ☐ Green, purple and gold
- ☐ Objects that people throw to the public
- ☐ People that wear costumes and masks
- ☐ The king of Mardi Gras
- ☐ Toy coins

USA

**Stop and Think!** Do people travel to attend festivals or celebrations in your country?

**1** 🎧²³ **Listen to the podcast and complete the information.**

beaches   Caribbean   **fortresses**   hotels   Old   Park

**1 Location**
- Puerto Rico, an **island** in the _____

**Destination: San Juan**

**2 Attractions**
- Historic Center: _____ San Juan
- Two _____
- El Morro and Castillo San Cristóbal

**3**
- Isla Verde and Ocean _____

**4 Accommodation**
- Old San Juan
- _____
- on the beach

**Glossary**

**podcast:** a pre-recorded audio program that you can download or listen to online

**fortress:** a large, strong building that defends a place, such as a city

**island:** a piece of land surrounded by water

2 **Create a podcast about a vacation destination.**
   **Follow the steps below:**
   1. Work in groups of four or five.
   2. Decide on a place you would like to talk about in your podcast.
   3. Use a mind map to help you organize the topics.

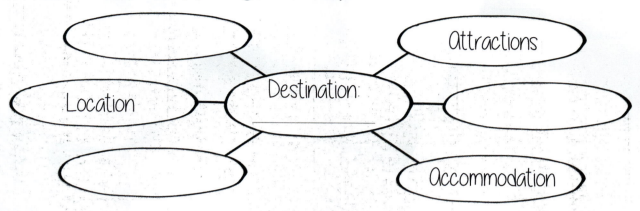

3 **Write an outline for your podcast using the diagram.**

4 **In your group, use the outline to write a script for your podcast.**
   **Follow these guidelines:**
   1. Everybody must participate.
   2. Consider the audience of your podcast: What can you do to attract your classmates' attention?
   3. Decide on the format of your podcast: an informal chat, or does each participant talk about a topic?
   4. Try to add some humor to your podcast.
   5. Review your text for grammar and spelling.
   6. Rehearse the script with your group.

5 **Record your podcast using a cell phone, tablet or computer. Then share it with your class.**

 **Stop and Think!** After listening to the podcasts, which vacation destination would you like to visit? Why?

# Review

## 1 Label the places.

He's at an _____ _____.

They are at a _____ _____.

They are at a _____ _____.

He's on a _____ _____.

She's on a _____ _____.

They're at an _____ _____.

She's at an _____ _____.

They're at a _____ _____.

## 2 Mark (✓) the correct adjectives.

1. That street market is so _____! There are too many people at the stalls.
   ☐ great   ☐ crowded

2. Alice thinks that aquariums are _____. She says fish aren't interesting at all…
   ☐ boring   ☐ fun

3. The zoo in our city is _____! The way the animals are treated is horrible.
   ☐ beautiful   ☐ terrible

4. The art museum is really _____. Visitors talk a lot there, they are never quiet!
   ☐ noisy   ☐ interesting

5. Do you think the amusement park is _____? Is it exciting and entertaining?
   ☐ fun   ☐ boring

## 3 Complete the description words with vowels.

1. b ___ ___ ___ t ___ f ___ l
2. b ___ r ___ n g
3. c r ___ w d ___ d
4. f ___ n
5. g r ___ ___ t
6. ___ n t ___ r ___ s t ___ n g
7. n ___ ___ s y
8. t ___ r r ___ b l ___

**4** **Look at the table. Then complete the sentences with *was, were, wasn't* or *weren't*.**

| Tourists sightseeing report – August 30 Tour guide responsible for the group: Harriet Stevens | | | |
|---|---|---|---|
| Name | Nationality | Attraction – 9 a.m. | Attraction – 2 p.m. |
| Akira and Mieko | Japanese | Museum of Modern Art | Sea Life Aquarium |
| Josh | American | County Street Market | Cocoa Beach |
| The Johnson family | British | Wild World Zoo | Museum of Modern Art |
| Hans | German | Sea Life Aquarium | Wild World Zoo |
| James and Steven | Australian | Cocoa Beach | ~~County Street Market~~ *Cocoa Beach* |

1. The Japanese tourists _____ at the Museum of Modern Art in the afternoon.
2. The family from the United Kingdom _____ at the Wild World Zoo in the morning.
3. The Australian tourists _____ at the beach in the afternoon.
4. The American tourist _____ at County Street Market in the morning.
5. The tourist from Germany _____ at the Wild World Zoo in the afternoon.

**5** **Complete the conversation.**

**TOUR MANAGER:** So, (1) _____ the tourists happy yesterday?

**HARRIET:** Yes, they (2) _____. They (3) _____ at different places in the city in the morning and in the afternoon.

**TOUR MANAGER:** Good! Where (4) _____ Akira and Mieko in the morning?

**HARRIET:** They were at the Museum of Modern Art. The exhibition (5) _____ great, in their opinion.

**TOUR MANAGER:** What about Josh? Where (6) _____ he?

**HARRIET:** Let me see… He (7) _____ at County Street Market in the morning.

**TOUR MANAGER:** And in the afternoon? (8) _____ he at the beach?

**HARRIET:** Yes, he (9) _____. He loves the beach!

**TOUR MANAGER:** (10) _____ James and Steven at the street market in the afternoon?

**HARRIET:** No, they (11) _____. They (12) _____ at the beach the whole day!

# Just for Fun

**1** Complete the crossword puzzle.

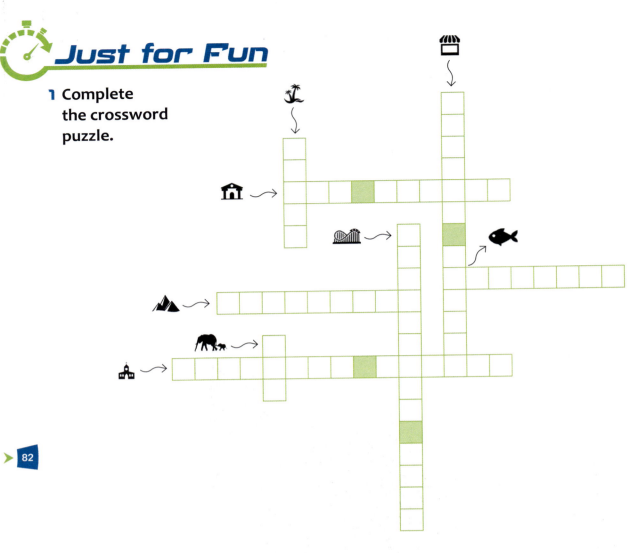

**2** Mark (✓) True or False. Then bet* on your answers.

| Fact | True | False | 1 – 10 points |
|---|---|---|---|
| 1. The largest airplane in the world is the Airbus A380. It accommodates 900 passengers. | | | |
| 2. There is an amusement park in Dubai about Ferrari, the Italian car race team and car manufacturer. | | | |
| 3. The highest mountain in the world is Mount Kilimanjaro, in Tanzania. | | | |
| 4. There is a beach covered in small pieces of glass in California, US. It's called "Glass Beach." | | | |
| 5. Millions of people visit the Museum of Modern Art, in New York, every year. It is the most visited museum in the world. | | | |
| 6. Floating markets are a popular tourist attraction in Thailand. Fruit and vegetables are sold on boats going up and down a river. | | | |
| *If you are certain that your answer is correct, bet 8 to 10 points. If you are not sure, bet fewer points. | | Score | |

**3** Check your answers. If you answered correctly, you win the points.

# Vocabulary

**1** 🎧24 **Listen and number the book genres.**

☐ Autobiography  ☐ Fantasy  ☐ Romance  ☐ Children's books

**2 Look at the movie genres. Read the movie reviews and circle the correct options.**

Science fiction    Action    Comedy    Animated

## THE MOVIE BLOG
Horror | Suspense | Action | Comedy | Romance

*Mars 2312* is a **comedy / science fiction** movie. Five astronauts travel to Mars on a space mission to the red planet. When they arrive at the planet, strange things happen!

*Heroes' Revenge* is the **action / animated** movie of the year! The superheroes we all love now fight the most popular villains of all time.

*Fun with the Spencers* tells the story of a family that moves to a new house and has funny problems. Fans of **science fiction / comedy** movies have a new film to love.

**3 Complete the sentences using the genres below.**

🧠 autobiography   😊 children's book   🐉 fantasy   ❤️ romance

---

yourbooksonline.net

## Tell us about the books you liked reading!

### Romeo and Juliet

**Sarah13** rated it ★ ★ ★ ★ ★

Romeo and Juliet *is my favorite* _____ *book. It's romantic, but also very* **interesting**—*you can't stop reading it!*

**BrianZ** replied 3h ago

*Interesting? That book is sooooooo* **boring**. *It's not interesting at all! I prefer a* _____ *book, like The Hobbit.*

Reply  👍
2d ago  44 likes

### The Diary of a Young Girl

**Ellen_BR** rated it ★ ★ ★ ★ ☆

The Diary of a Young Girl *is the best* _____.
*Anne Frank's story is really* **sad**—*it made me feel unhappy and emotional!*

**BookWormJake** replied 21h ago

*Did you read I Am Malala? It's kind of sad, too, but also* **inspirational**—*now I want to change the world!*

**Lovely_Aileen** replied 15h ago

*Another inspirational book is The Little Prince. Some people think it is a simple* _____, *but it's really poetic!*

Reply  👍
3d ago  73 likes

M ▣ t f ⊕  G+1

---

**4 🎧²⁵ Listen and number the adjectives.**

1. *The Diary of a Young Girl*
2. *Mars 2312*
3. *Romeo and Juliet*
4. *Fun with the Spencers*
5. *The Little Prince*

☐ boring
☐ funny
☐ sad
☐ interesting
☐ inspirational

> **Guess What!**
> The seven books in the *Harry Potter* series have sold over 450 million copies worldwide!

⏱ 2 min  **5 Think Fast!** In your notebook, write a movie or book title for each genre.

# Grammar

**Roald Dahl (1916-1990)**

Roald Dahl was born in the UK in 1916. His parents were from Norway. He visit**ed** his grandparents in Norway on summer vacations. Dahl studi**ed** at a famous school, but he wasn't a good student. He always want**ed** to visit other countries.

Dahl work**ed** with the Shell Oil Company in London and in Africa. Then in World War II, he was a fighter pilot. One day, his plane crash**ed** in North Africa. After that, Dahl work**ed** in Washington, D.C.

Dahl also publish**ed** stories and articles for magazines. Dahl creat**ed** his first story for children, The Gremlins, in 1942, for Walt Disney. Dahl publish**ed** 17 children's books.

**1** Look at the biography. Is it about the present or the past? _____

**2** Read the information about Roald Dahl. In your notebook, answer the questions.
1. Where were Roald Dahl's grandparents from?
2. Where was the plane crash?
3. What was his first story for children?

**3** Complete the chart using the verbs from the article.

| visit | → | _____ | study | → | _____ |
| want | → | _____ | work | → | _____ |
| crash | → | _____ | publish | → | _____ |
| create | → | _____ | | | |

**Glossary**

fighter

crash

pilot

**publish:** prepare a book or story to sell it

**4** Read the biography and circle the past forms of the verbs.

### Biography - Antoine de Saint Exupéry (1900-1944)

In the 1920s and 1930s, Saint Exupéry was an airmail pilot, a **journalist** and a writer in France. Later he lived in Argentina, where he met his wife Consuelo. In World War II, Saint-Exupéry was a military pilot. In 1940, he went to the US. There he wrote his most famous book: *The Little Prince*. After that, he returned to Europe in 1943.

On July 31, 1944, Saint-Exupéry went on a mission in his plane and **disappeared**. Nobody saw the writer or his plane again. Finally, in May 2000, a **diver** found parts of a World War II airplane in the Mediterranean Sea. It was Saint-Exupéry's plane.

*The Little Prince* is available in 250 languages. Saint-Exupéry wrote the story and made the illustrations.

**5** Complete the chart using verbs from the biography.

| meet → _____ | go → went | write → _____ |
| see → _____ | find → _____ | make → _____ |

**6** Complete the sentences. Use the past forms of the verbs.

1. Saint-Exupéry _____ (go) to Argentina in 1929.
2. He _____ (be) the director of *Aeroposta Argentina*, the first airline company in the country.
3. He first _____ (meet) his wife Consuelo in Buenos Aires in 1930.
4. He _____ (write) about his experiences in Argentina for his book *Night Flight*.

**7 Think Fast!** Write two things Dahl and Saint-Exupéry have in common.

**G**lossary

**journalist:** a person who writes for a newspaper or magazine

**disappear:** to go away completely or to stop being visible

diver

# Listening & Writing

a girls' school, Pakistan

1 Look at the pictures. Say what happened to Malala Yousafzai.

2  26 Listen to Malala's story to check your ideas.

3 Read the sentences. Then listen again and write the numbers.

**Be Strategic!**
Pay special attention to dates and words such as *when*, *then* and *after* (*that*). They help you understand the sequence of events in a story.

Taliban invasion

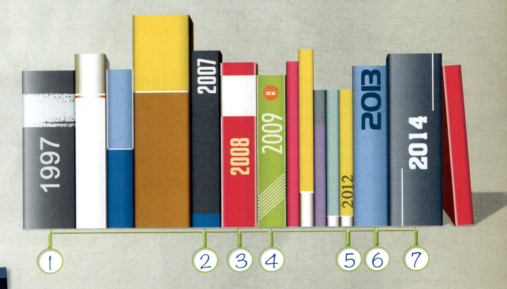

▸ 88

gunman

☐ A gunman attacked Malala.
☐ Malala published her autobiography.
[1] Malala was born.
☐ She started a blog about her life in Pakistan. The **Taliban** closed girls' schools.
☐ Malala won the Nobel Peace Prize.
☐ The Taliban invaded Swat Valley.
[4] Thanks to Malala, the Taliban opened the schools again.

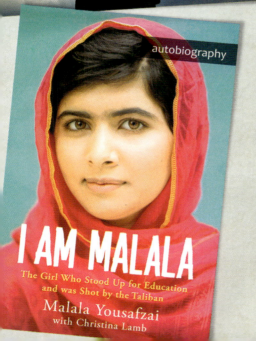
autobiography

Nobel Peace Prize

## Anne Frank (1929 – 1945)

Amsterdam, Holland

Birthday: June 12
Place of birth: Frankfurt, Germany
Lived: Amsterdam, Holland
Place of death: Bergen-Belsen Concentration Camp, Germany
Book: The Diary of a Young Girl
Parents: Otto and Edith Frank
Sister: Margot

- June 1942 – Anne Frank got a diary for her birthday and started writing.
- July 1942 – Anne and her family started living in a secret place to hide from the Nazis.
- August 1944 – The Nazis found Anne and her family and took them to concentration camps.
- March 1945 – Anne died of typhus.
- 1947 – Anne's father published Anne's diary.

Anne Frank

89

**4** Read and circle **T** (True) or **F** (False).

1. Anne always lived in Germany.              T    F
2. She first wrote in her diary in 1942.      T    F
3. Anne died in a concentration camp.         T    F
4. The family lived in a secret location for four years.   T    F

**5** In your notebook, write a short biography of Anne Frank using *When*, *Then* and *After that*.

Nazis

Anne Frank was born on June 12, 1929 in Frankfurt, Germany. She lived in Amsterdam, Holland. Her parents were…

concentration camp

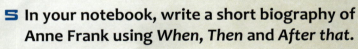
**Stop and Think!** What can we learn from the life stories of Malala and Anne Frank?

**Glossary**
**Taliban:** a fundamentalist Islamic movement active in areas of Pakistan and Afghanistan
**typhus:** an infectious disease

# culture

HOME • TRAVEL BLOG • GUIDES • COMMUNITY

Morocco

## Dan's ADVENTURES in Africa

### The Storytellers of Morocco

Aug 18  /  Posted by Dan Shultz  /  12 comments  /  Marrakesh, Morocco

Yesterday afternoon, I was in Marrakesh, Morocco, with my parents and their Moroccan friend, Ahbed. We saw snake charmers and magicians on Jemaa el-Fna, the famous square.

When an old man arrived, people made a circle around him. He was a storyteller. Ahbed explained that storytelling is an important part of Moroccan culture and that people really respect storytellers. The stories usually include a moral aspect.

The old man **spoke** in Arabic, and Ahbed translated the story into English for me. It was about the creation of the Sahara Desert.

Then we went to a coffee shop. Old storytellers were teaching young students there, so that the tradition doesn't disappear.

---

**1 Match the captions to the pictures.**

1. Evening on the main square
2. A storyteller at Jemaa el-Fna
3. The city of Marrakesh in Morocco
4. Moroccan food

**2 Read the blog post and answer the questions in your notebook.**

1. Where was Dan yesterday?
2. Who did he listen to?
3. What was the story about?
4. Why do storytellers have students?

**3** 🎧²⁷ **Listen to the storyteller. Order the events in the story.**

☐ The people said a **grain of sand** wouldn't make a difference.

☐ People on earth **told lies** every day, and the spirit threw grains of sand on earth.

☒ 1 The earth was a beautiful place. Nobody told lies.

☐ The grains of sand formed the Sahara Desert. An oasis shows the original garden, because there are people who don't **tell lies**.

☐ The spirit called all the people on earth—every time someone told a lie, he would **throw** a grain of sand onto earth.

☐ A person told a lie. It was the end of man's innocence.

**Glossary**
**spoke:** past of speak
**tell a lie:** say something that is not true
**grain of sand:** a small particle of beaches and deserts

throw

**Based on:** *The Birth of the Sahara*, by Ahmed Tamiicha, in: Richard Hamilton (2011), *The Last Storytellers: Tales from the Heart of Morocco*, I.B. Tauris & Co.

**4 Think Fast!** Name three popular stories in your culture.
1 min

**Stop and Think!** How important are oral stories in your country?

91

# Project

**1** Look at the timeline. Then read the sentences and circle *T* (True) or *F* (False).

1. There aren't any visual elements in the timeline.   T   F
2. The events in the timeline are in chronological order.   T   F
3. All the events in John's life are included in the timeline.   T   F
4. The sentences are very long and give many details.   T   F

 **2 Think Fast!** Where does the extra paper go?

3 Create your own timeline and present it to your classmates.

a memento

## How to Create a Clothesline Timeline

Preparing your text and images:

1. Plan your timeline: write a list with events in chronological order.
   - Mention the years.
   - Include only events that are important to you.
   - Write the verbs in the past simple.
2. Write each event on a piece of paper. Include the dates.
3. Include pictures or drawings.
4. You can use some **mementos** to symbolize an event.

Forming your timeline:

The string is your timeline. Use the clothespins to fasten the sheets you prepared at home to the string. Place the events in chronological order.

clothespins

Presenting your timeline:

1. Work in groups of six students.
2. Share the events of your timeline with your classmates. Ask two classmates to hold each end of the string while you talk.

string

**Glossary**

**lost:** the past of *lose*: not have any more

**memento:** a small object you keep to remind you of something or someone

# Review

**1 Complete the words using vowels.**

| Book Genres | Movie Genres |
|---|---|
| 1. __ __ t __ b __ __ g r __ p h y | 5. __ c t __ __ n |
| 2. c h __ l d r __ n's  b __ __ k | 6. __ n __ m __ t __ d |
| 3. f __ n t __ s y | 7. c __ m __ d y |
| 4. r __ m __ n c __ | 8. s c __ __ n c __  f __ c t __ __ n |

**2 Label the book genres.**

_____  _____  _____  _____

**3 Mark (✓) the correct words to complete the sentences.**

1. _____ movies are fun and humorous. They make people laugh.
   ☐ Action          ☐ Comedy

2. _____ movies usually imagine life in the future, or developments in science, like time travel.
   ☐ Animated        ☐ Science fiction

3. _____ movies don't have real people. They have computer-generated characters.
   ☐ Animated        ☐ Comedy

4. _____ movies usually have a hero. They can be violent sometimes.
   ☐ Comedy          ☐ Action

**4 Correct the sentences. Rewrite the underlined words.**

1. *Love in a Rainy Afternoon* is such a <u>funny</u> book! I cried a lot  when I read it.
   _____

2. This movie is so <u>interesting</u> 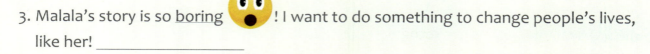! Let's watch something else...
   _____

3. Malala's story is so <u>boring</u> ! I want to do something to change people's lives, like her! _____

5 **Complete the sentences using the past forms of the verbs below.**

crash  create  study  want  write

1. We _____ world literature and movies in this unit.
2. Shakespeare _____ about many famous historical characters.
3. Roald Dahl _____ stories for children and adults.
4. Dahl and Exupéry _____ their airplanes in the 20th century.
5. In his book about Katherines, John Green _____ to explain love and math.

6 **Complete the chart with the past forms. Then write R (Regular) or I (Irregular).**

|  | Past form | R / I |  | Past form | R / I |
|---|---|---|---|---|---|
| 1. create | _____ | ___ | 8. meet | _____ | ___ |
| 2. disappear | _____ | ___ | 9. see | _____ | ___ |
| 3. explain | _____ | ___ | 10. start | _____ | ___ |
| 4. find | _____ | ___ | 11. study | _____ | ___ |
| 5. go | _____ | ___ | 12. visit | _____ | ___ |
| 6. live | _____ | ___ | 13. work | _____ | ___ |
| 7. make | _____ | ___ | 14. write | _____ | ___ |

7 **Complete the biography using the past forms of the verbs.**

1. J. R. R. Tolkien _____ (be) a British writer and academic.
2. Ronald _____ (be) born in South Africa on January 3, 1892.
3. He and his family _____ (go) to England when he _____ (be) a child.
4. He _____ (be) a lieutenant in World War I.
5. Tolkien _____ (work) as a professor at Oxford University for many years.
6. He _____ (make) over 100 illustrations for The Hobbit.
7. He _____ (write) the three books of The Lord of the Rings trilogy in the 1950s.

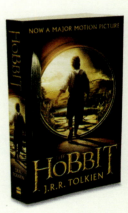

# Just for Fun

**1** Unscramble the book and movie genres. Then use the numbered letters to find the mystery genre.

h a y p u i b o o g a r t   ☐☐☐☐☐☐☐☐☐☐☐☐ (books)
                                              9

f y a s n t a   ☐☐☐☐☐☐☐ (books)
                 8      1

c o e n a r m   ☐☐☐☐☐☐☐ (books)
                    13    2

n c r e i d l h's   ☐☐☐☐☐☐'☐ (books)
                     6  3     5

c o y m e d   ☐☐☐☐☐☐ (movies)
              10    4

n a m i t d a e   ☐☐☐☐☐☐☐☐ (movies)
                      12  11  7

n i o t a c   ☐☐☐☐☐☐ (movies)
                  14

☐☐☐☐☐☐☐  ☐☐☐☐☐☐☐
1 2 3 4 5 6 7   8 9 10 11 12 13 14

**2** Complete the quote by Malala Yousafzai. Only copy letters from the same column.

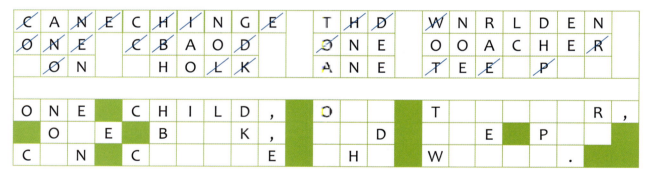

**3** Solve the crossword puzzle using the past forms of the verbs. Then answer the question.

**Down** ↓
1. see
2. find
4. speak (page 90)
5. meet

**Across** →
3. write
5. make
6. lose (page 92)
7. go

What do the verb forms in the puzzle have in common?
They are all _____ verbs.

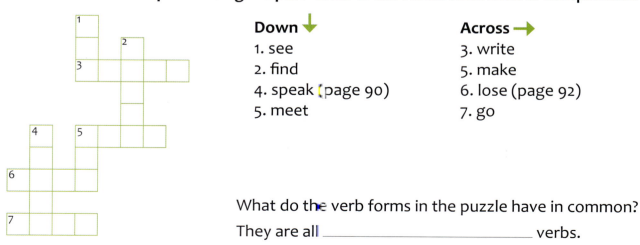

# Vocabulary

**1** 🎧²⁸ **Listen and number the professions.**

## Six Professions That Can Change the World

What do you want to be?

☐ Teacher

☐ Scientist

☐ Nurse

☐ Journalist

☐ Social worker

☐ Artist

**Guess What!**
According to UNESCO, the world will need an extra 5.1 million teachers to teach all the kids in lower secondary education by 2030.

**2** 🎧²⁸ **Number the descriptions using the professions. Then listen again to check your answers.**

1. _____ create or perform in public.
2. _____ help create new medicines.
3. _____ present information as a story.
4. _____ help people learn.
5. _____ paint, make music, take photos, etc.
6. _____ work for magazines, TV, etc.
7. _____ help families.
8. _____ study the world.
9. _____ administer medication.

3 Write the professions.

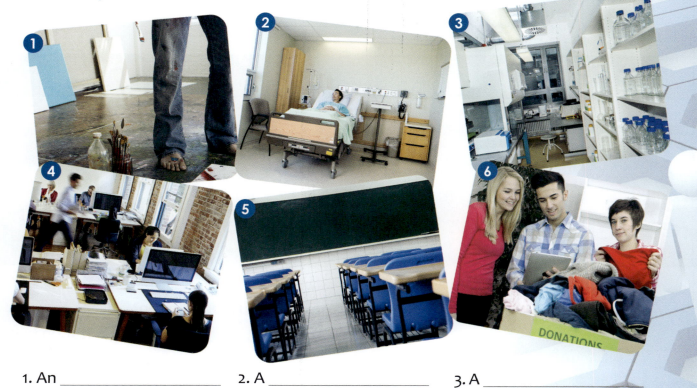

1. An _____ works in a studio.
2. A _____ works at a hospital.
3. A _____ works in a laboratory.
4. A _____ works in an office and also on the streets.
5. A _____ normally works at a school.
6. A _____ _____ can work at a community center.

4 🎧²⁹ Listen and write the professions.

**Florence Nightingale**
(1820 – 1910) was a
_____.

**Marie Curie**
(1867 – 1934) was a
_____.

**Anne Sullivan**
(1866 – 1936) was a
_____.

5 Think Fast! What do the people in Activity 4 have in common?

**1** Complete the interview with the verbs in past.

joined   learned   made   talked

# Meet Our Volunteers
This month's volunteer: Zach Kowalsky (13)

**GoGreen:** When **did** you **join** GoGreen?

**Zach:** I (1) _____ the organization two years ago. A volunteer came to my school and he (2) _____ about GoGreen.

**GoGreen:** Why **did** you **become** a volunteer?

**Zach:** I think we all need to help the planet.

**GoGreen:** Zach, **did** you **plant** trees from the start?

**Zach:** No, I **didn't**. First I (3) _____ about different kinds of trees.

**GoGreen:** So what **did** you **do** after the classes?

**Zach:** I helped other volunteers.

**GoGreen:** And **did** you **like** the work?

**Zach:** Yes, I **did**! I **didn't get** bored. And I (4) _____ good friends, too.

**2** Write two more questions for Zach. Use the past simple.

1. A: What _____ you **do**? B: I planted trees.
2. A: _____ you **like** the work? B: Yes, I _____. / No, I _____.

 **3 Think Fast!** In your notebook, write two more questions for Zach using the past simple.

**G**lossary

**join:** become a member of a group

**4** Unscramble the questions. Then answer and write your score.

## How did you help to change the world?

1. how / you / get to school / did / yesterday / ?

_____

| | | Me | My partner |
|---|---|---|---|
| | I walked. / I rode my bike. | | |
| | By public transportation (bus, train, subway… ). | | |
| | By car. | | |

2. where / you / throw your garbage / did / yesterday / ?

_____

| | | Me | My partner |
|---|---|---|---|
| | I threw it in recycling bins, separating the trash. | | |
| | I threw it in a bin, but I didn't separate it. | | |
| | I don't remember… maybe on the street? | | |

3. you / do any volunteer work / did / last year / ?

_____

| | Yes, I did. | | No, I didn't. | | |
|---|---|---|---|---|---|

4. you / turn off your computer / yesterday / did / ?

_____

| | Yes, I did. | | No, I didn't. | | |
|---|---|---|---|---|---|

5. you / say "thank you" / this morning / did / to someone / ?

_____

| | Yes, I did. | | No, I didn't. | | |
|---|---|---|---|---|---|

**5** Work with a partner. Ask and answer the questions in the quiz.

**6** Add up your scores and check your result.

| 20 – 25 | You really contribute to change in the world! Great job! |
|---|---|
| 12 – 19 | You are helping to change the world, but you can do better. Try to care more for the planet and for other people! |
| 0 – 11 | You should stop and think about your actions. Maybe you aren't paying much attention to the world and to the people around you… |

TeensChangeTheWorld.org

# Reading & Speaking

**1** Read the article quickly. Mark (✓) the purpose of the text.

1. ☐ To persuade
2. ☐ To inform
3. ☐ To entertain

**Teen Profile**
**Name:** Natalie Prabhu
**Age:** 13
**From:** Bristol, United Kingdom
**Contribution:** *ReMind,* a watch that **reminds** elderly people to take their medicine.

## TEEN HEROES

*Let's learn about Natalie and her invention.*

**TCTW:** Who was the inspiration for your app?
**NATALIE:** My grandfather. He often forgets to take his medicine.
**TCTW:** Who helped you?
**NATALIE:** Ms. Williams, my science teacher, helped me with the concept. My mother is an engineer, and we built a prototype together.
**TCTW:** When did you build it?
**NATALIE:** Two months ago. It was a lot of work!
**TCTW:** Did you need much money to do that?
**NATALIE:** Not really. We used a smartwatch. It cost $200. We reprogrammed some settings. My grandfather wears it every day. Now we need investors for the project to improve our app.

**2** How did these people contribute to *ReMind*? Match the parts of the sentences.

Natalie's mother

Natalie's grandfather

Ms. Williams

**Be Strategic!**
Texts are written to *persuade* you (e.g., advertising that makes you buy something), *inform* (articles that tell you something new), or *entertain* (stories that are interesting).

helped Natalie create the concept for the app.

built the prototype for the app with Natalie.

inspired Natalie to create *ReMind.*

**G**lossary
**remind:** help someone remember something

**3** Read and answer with a partner: Who is Matt's hero? Why?

Matt

Madison

My older sister, Madison, is my hero. She had cancer when she was 16 years old. She had surgery and chemotherapy.
Fortunately, she survived cancer! Madison is my personal hero because she is very brave and strong. She taught me to enjoy life in difficult moments.

**4** Who is *your* personal hero? Complete the chart.

| Name: | |
|---|---|
| Relationship: | |
| Occupation: | |
| Inspiring action/situation: | |
| Why the person is your hero: | |

**5** Work in small groups. Ask your partners about their heroes. Use your notes from Activity 4 to talk about yours.

Who's your hero?

My grandfather, Thomas. He was an architect.

Why is he your hero?

Because he always helped people.

 **Stop and Think!** What can you learn from personal heroes?

## Culture

# TANZANIA and SWAHILI

**1** Read about a girl's experience in Tanzania. Mark (✓) the best title for the text.

1. My Visit to Mount Kilimanjaro National Park ☐
2. How to Plant Trees in a Forest ☐
3. A Memorable Experience ☐

*Jambo!* My name's Chloe and I'm 13. I spent one month on a volunteer program in Tanzania last year, in a village near Mount Kilimanjaro. The other volunteers and I planted native trees in a **forest** nearby. We also studied the impact of human activity on the forest's ecosystem. On weekends, we went on a safari in the Serengeti National Park, and we visited the Ngorongoro Conservation Area and the beautiful beaches in Zanzibar. I learned some **Swahili**, too!

Tanzania is a fantastic place! The people are friendly and its culture and **wildlife** are fascinating. It was the best experience of my life.

**2** Complete the information with words from the text.

1. a girl's name: _____
2. a country: _____
3. a national park: _____

**Glossary**

**jambo:** *hello* in Swahili
**forest:** a large area covered with trees
**Swahili:** an African language
**wildlife:** animals and plants living in natural conditions

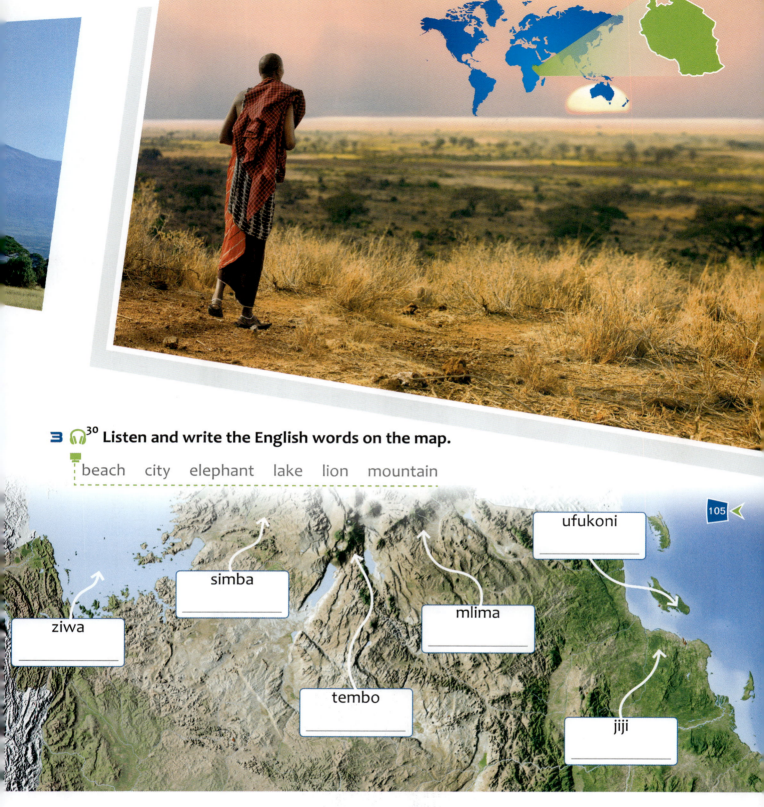

3 🎧³⁰ **Listen and write the English words on the map.**

beach   city   elephant   lake   lion   mountain

ufukoni _____

simba _____

ziwa _____

mlima _____

tembo _____

jiji _____

4 **Read and answer the questions with a partner.**
   1. Tanzania has 125 languages—two official ones (English and Swahili) and 123 minority languages. Are there any minority languages in your country? What are they?
   2. Most Tanzanians are bilingual. Do most people in your country speak two languages? Which languages?

 **Stop and Think!**   How do languages connect people?

# Help Your Community

**1 Write the steps in order. Refer to page 102 if necessary.**

___ Natalie looks for investors to improve the app.
_1_ Natalie Pradhu's grandfather forgets to take his medicine.
___ Natalie's grandfather uses the prototype. It works!
___ Natalie wants to help him.
___ She asks her mother to help her.
___ She talks to her science teacher.
___ They complete the prototype.

**2 Read and mark (✓) the sentences that are true for your community. Then add two more sentences.**

___ Streets or parks are dirty.
___ Elderly people need help with shopping, gardening, etc.
___ New students at school need a **buddy**.
___ _____
___ _____

**3** **Form small groups. Answer the questions.**

1. What is a problem in your community that you want to solve?
_____
_____
_____

2. What steps are there in your plan?
_____
_____

3. Who is on your team? What is each member planning to do?
_____
_____

**4** **Present your plan to the class.**

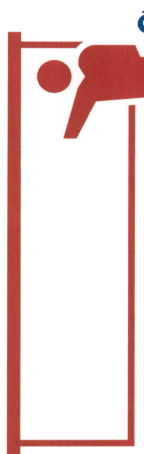

**5** **Present the results of your actions in one month.**

**buddy:** a partner to do things with, a friend

# Review

**1 Complete the puzzle with six professions. Then complete the sentence using the word in the green box.**

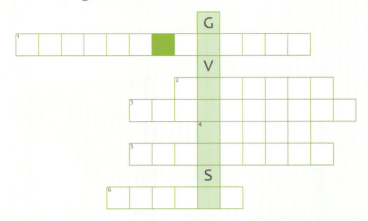

A g ___ v ___ ___ ___ ___ s ___ is a woman who teaches a child at the child's house.

**2 Label the workplaces.**

_____   _____   _____

_____   _____   _____

**3 Read the sentences and correct the workplaces.**

1. Nurses work in art studios. _____
2. Scientists work at community centers. _____
3. Social workers work at laboratories. _____
4. Artists work in offices. _____
5. Journalists work in schools. _____
6. Teachers work at hospitals. _____

**4 Match the questions to the answers.**

1. ___ Was Madame Curie always a scientist?
2. ___ Where did Marie Curie study?
3. ___ Did she study physics?
4. ___ Why did she receive the Nobel Prize?
5. ___ When did she win the Nobel Prize?

a. Because of her work on radioactivity.
b. No, she wasn't. She was a governess first.
c. She won the prize in 1903 and 1911.
d. Yes, she did. And mathematics, too.
e. She studied at a university in Paris.

**5 Unscramble the questions.**

1. live / did / Marie Curie / in France all her life / ?

_____

No, she didn't. She was born in Poland.

2. move / to France / why / did / she / ?

_____

Because women couldn't attend university in Poland in the 19th century.

3. when / she / at the Sorbonne / start / did / ?

_____

She entered the Sorbonne in 1891.

4. Marie Curie / have / did / any children / ?

_____

Yes, she had two daughters. Irene, the oldest, was also a scientist.

5. did / where / die / she / ?

_____

She died in France, in 1934. She was very sick from the exposure to radiation during her life.

**6 Change the sentences into negative sentences (–) or questions (?).**

1. My mother studied at Harvard University. (–)

_____

2. Alice lived in Spain for three years. (?)

_____

3. Tyler went on vacation last month. (–)

_____

4. Sam's dad worked last Saturday. (?)

_____

# Just for Fun

**1** Write the professions based on the pictures.

**2** Write the past form of the verbs using the letters in the table.

1. be – _____
2. go – _____
3. have – _____
4. make – _____
5. meet – _____
6. ride – _____
7. take – _____
8. throw – _____

| A | D | E | H |
|---|---|---|---|
| K | M | N | O |
| R | S | T | W |

**3** Cross out one extra word in each question. Write the words. Then write the words in order to form the mystery question.

1. Did you get do to school by car yesterday? _____
2. Where did you recycle the what plastic bottles? _____
3. How many plants did you plant last week yesterday? _____
4. Did Mia go did to the community center on Sunday? _____
5. When did you join the volunteer you team? _____

Mystery question:
_____

# How do we spend our free time?

8

# Vocabulary

**1 Look and complete the activities.**

room | dishes | dog | friends | movie | park | trash | video games

## Chores

1. walk the _____
2. do the _____
3. clean your _____
4. take out the _____

## Fun Activities

5. watch a _____
6. hang out with _____
7. play _____
8. go to the _____

## 2 Mark (✓) when you do these activities.

| Activity | Mon | Tue | Wed | Thu | Fri | Sat | Sun |
|---|---|---|---|---|---|---|---|
| Clean your room | | | | | | | |
| Do the dishes | | | | | | | |
| Go to the park | | | | | | | |
| Hang out with friends | | | | | | | |
| Play video games | | | | | | | |
| Take out the trash | | | | | | | |
| Walk the dog | | | | | | | |
| Watch a movie | | | | | | | |

**Stop and Think!** Share your information with a classmate. Who does the most chores?

## 3 🎧³¹ Listen and circle the correct emoticon. Then complete the sentences.

1. Mel is 🙂 🙁 _____
2. Jessica is 😠 🙂 _____
3. Thomas and Finn are 😀 🙂 _____
4. Lucas is 😐 🙂 _____
5. Josh is 😀 🙂 _____

angry · bored · excited · happy · nervous · sad · scared · tired

**Guess What!** More than 50% of teenagers in the US text their friends every day.

## 4 Read and write an adjective. How do you feel?

1. You are walking the dog at night when you hear a strange noise. _____
2. You have a fight with your mom. _____
3. You are doing your homework. It's very difficult. _____
4. You are hanging out with your best friend. _____

◀ 113

#  Grammar

**1** 🎧³² **Listen and write *Aiden* and/or *John*.**

Aiden,
These are the chores you and John have to do this week:
- clean your room _____
- walk Rufus _____
- do the dishes _____
- go to the supermarket with me _____

We'll talk about the division of the chores when I get back home tonight.
Love,
Dad

### Have to

Aiden and John **have to clean** their room.
John **has to walk** Rufus.

 114

**2 Circle the correct form.**

1. Oh, no! I **have to / has to** take out the trash and it's raining!
2. My little sister helps around the house. She **have to / has to** clean her room.
3. My father hates to do the dishes, but he **have to / has to** do them every night.
4. We **have to / has to** go to the supermarket with our parents every week.
5. Brandon and Alex **have to / has to** walk the family dogs in the afternoon.

**3 Write four sentences about the chores you and people in your family have to do.**

| clean my room | clean the kitchen | |
| take out the trash | do the dishes | mother   father |
| go to the supermarket | walk the dog | brother   sister |

1. _____
2. _____
3. _____
4. _____

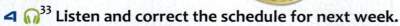

**4** 🎧³³ **Listen and correct the schedule for next week.**

| Aiden's schedule | Morning | Afternoon | Evening |
|---|---|---|---|
| Monday 5 | School | Soccer practice | Do homework |
| Tuesday 6 | School | Guitar lessons | Do the dishes |
| Wednesday 7 | School | Soccer practice | Do homework |
| Thursday 8 | School | Guitar lessons | Do the dishes |
| Friday 9 | School | Free! | Free! |
| Saturday 10 |  | Go to the park with friends / Go to the supermarket | Clean our room |
| Sunday 11 | Free! | Free! | Free! |

**5 Complete the sentences with the correct verbs.**

> do   go   play

| | Going to – Future |
|---|---|
|  | 1. Aiden **is going to** _____ soccer on Monday. |
| **Negative** | 2. He **isn't going to** _____ homework on Saturday afternoon. |
| **Questions** | 3. When **is** Aiden **going to** _____ to the park with his friends? |
|  | 4. **Is** he **going to** _____ to school on Saturday? **No**, he **isn't**. |

**6 Look and answer the questions about Aiden's schedule.**

1. When is Aiden going to play soccer?
   _____

2. What is Aiden going to do on Tuesday and Thursday afternoon?
   _____

3. Is Aiden going to do the dishes on Tuesday and Thursday evening?
   _____

4. Is Aiden going to the supermarket on Friday afternoon?
   _____

5. When are Aiden and John going to clean their room?
   _____

# Reading & Speaking

**1** Mark (✓) the kind of information you expect in party invitations.

1. The **host**'s name ☐
2. The date and time of the party ☐
3. The names of the people invited ☐
4. The type of party ☐
5. The location of the party ☐

**2** Read the invitation and check your answers.

### Madison's Pool Party Surprise!

Join us to celebrate Madison's 13th birthday!
Don't forget your swimsuit, **flip-flops** and **towel**!

When? Saturday, July 1
What time? 2 p.m.
Where? Madison's house - 345 Brooke St.
Shh... it's a surprise!
Contact? Ava and Hailey

**3** Imagine you received the invitation. Answer the questions.

1. What kind of party is it?
   _____

2. Is it Ava and Hailey's birthday party?
   _____

3. What do you need to take to participate in the party?
   _____

4. When is the party going to take place?
   _____

5. Is the party going to happen at a club?
   _____

6. Can you talk to Madison about the party?
   _____

**Be Strategic!**
To find out specific information, think about the type of word that will provide the answer, for example, a name or a date.

**Glossary**
**host:** the person who invites others to a party

flip flops

towel

116

4 🎧³⁴ **Listen and read along.**

### Inviting Someone

A: Invite your classmate.

> Would you like to go to Madison's birthday party?

B: Ask when the party is.

> When is it?

A: Say when it is.

> It's on Saturday, July 1st.

### Accepting an Invitation

B: Ask what time the party is.

> Sure, I'd love to. What time?

A: Answer Student B's question.

> At 2 p.m.

B: Ask where the party is.

> And where is it?

A: Answer Student B's question. Say what type of party it is.

> At Madison's house. It's a pool party.

React and discuss the details.

> Great!

> But don't tell Madison, OK? It's a surprise party.

> Of course!

### Rejecting an Invitation

B: Explain why you can't go.

> Sorry, I can't. I'm going to travel with my parents on Friday.

A: Say it's too bad.

> That's too bad… Maybe next time.

A & B: React and discuss the details.

> Sure.

> But don't tell Madison, OK? It's a surprise party.

> OK!

5 **In pairs, practice the conversations.**

6 **Work in small groups. Take turns inviting to a party and accepting or rejecting invitations.**

Lights, camera, action!
Join us for a night on the red carpet!

When? Friday, June 30th
What time? 7 p.m.
Where? At the Community Center
Dress up as a movie star or character!

Green Valley Middle School invites teachers, students and parents to its annual End-of-Term Picnic!

When? Sunday, July 2nd
What time? From 11 a.m. to 4 p.m.
Where? At Green Park (near the lake)
Join us for great food and fun!

## Culture

# HAWAIIAN LUAUS

In Hawaii, a luau is a traditional party to celebrate an important event with music, dance and food.

Many years ago, men and women didn't eat together in Hawaii. King Kamehameha II changed that in the 19th century, and he organized the first luau as a celebration for men *and* women. The word *luau* comes from one of the traditional dishes, made with leaves of taro plants, meat and coconut milk.

Luaus are organized outdoors: at a garden or on the beach. Hawaiian women dance the hula, while musicians play the ukulele and other instruments. Besides eating *lūʻau*, people eat poi (a paste made of taro leaves), roasted pork and fish.

**1 Think Fast!** Look at the pictures. In your notebook, write 10 words of things you see.

**2** Read the article. Then match.

1. The 19th century
2. King Kamehameha II
3. A traditional dish
4. Beaches and gardens
5. *Poi* and roasted pork

☐ permitted men and women to eat together.
☐ are traditional dishes served at luaus.
☐ was the inspiration for the name *luau*.
☐ is the period when Hawaiians started having luaus.
☐ are some places where luaus happen.

**3** Label the five pictures above using the highlighted words.

 **Stop and Think!** Are Hawaiians always on vacation? Why do you think so?

**4** Organize a luau. Copy the table in your notebook and write who does what.

Make the invitations        Shop for food and drinks      Prepare food
Dance the hula at the party  Play music at the party       Clean up after the luau

| Tasks | People Responsible |
|---|---|
|  |  |

**Guess What!**
The menu at King Kamehameha II's luau in 1847 included 2245 coconuts, 4000 taro plants, 482 bowls of *poi*, 3125 salted fish, 1820 fresh fish and 271 pigs.

# Project

**1 Look at the text below and mark (✓) the text type.**

☐ a survey – an activity where you ask the same question to different people

☐ an article – a text that informs people about a certain topic, or topics

## Free-time activities

**Question #1:** How many hours a week is your free time? (Ignore sleeping hours.)

|  | Respondent 1 | Respondent 2 | Respondent 3 | Respondent 4 |
|---|---|---|---|---|
| 0 – 10 hours/week | ✓ |  |  |  |
| 11 – 20 hours/week |  |  |  | ✓ |
| 21 – 30 hours/week |  | ✓ | ✓ |  |
| more than 30 hours/week |  |  |  |  |

**Question #2:** Are you happy with the amount of free time in your week?

|  | Respondent 1 | Respondent 2 | Respondent 3 | Respondent 4 |
|---|---|---|---|---|
| Yes |  |  | ✓ | ✓ |
| No | ✓ | ✓ |  |  |

**Question #3:** What is your favorite free-time activity?

|  | Respondent 1 | Respondent 2 | Respondent 3 | Respondent 4 |
|---|---|---|---|---|
| Hanging out with friends |  |  |  |  |
| Reading books | ✓ |  |  |  |
| Surfing the Internet |  | ✓ |  |  |
| Going to the park |  |  | ✓ |  |
| Other: |  |  |  | *Play soccer* |

**Question #4:** Who do you spend most of your free time with?

|  | Respondent 1 | Respondent 2 | Respondent 3 | Respondent 4 |
|---|---|---|---|---|
| With friends |  | ✓ |  | ✓ |
| With family |  |  | ✓ |  |
| With a pet |  |  |  |  |
| Alone | ✓ |  |  |  |

**2 Circle *T* (True) or *F* (False).**

1. There are questions and possible answers in a survey.     T     F
2. *Respondents* ask the questions in a survey.     T     F
3. You write the answers in complete sentences.     T     F

3 **Work in small groups. Create and carry out a survey.**

**Step 1:** Choose a topic for your survey.

Types of free-time activities your classmates do or like   Plans for next week
Chores your classmates have to do at home   Vacation plans

**Step 2:** In your notebook, create a survey. Write four questions and possible answers.

**Step 3:** Each classmate interviews four different people. Ask the questions and record the answers.

**Step 4:** Put together the results of the surveys in your group. Use graphs to organize the information.

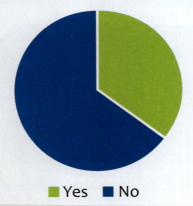

4 **Now present the results of your survey to the class.**

Our survey is about _____.
                              topic

Our first / second / third / fourth question was _____.
                                                              question

_____ answered _____.
   number of people                              possible answer

Our conclusion is that _____.
                                your conclusion

# Review

**1 Match the parts.**

1. clean ☐ the dog
2. do ☐ the trash
3. walk ☐ your room
4. take out ☐ the dishes

5. go ☐ video games
6. hang out with ☐ a movie
7. play ☐ to the park
8. watch ☐ friends

**2 Number the pictures using the phrases from Activity 1.**

**3 Label the emoticons.**

1. _____  2. _____  3. _____  4. _____

5. _____  6. _____  7. _____  8. _____

**4 Complete the sentences with *have to* or *has to*. Then say the sentences.**

1. Matt and Mia can't go to the 🌳 now. They _____ clean the 🧊.
2. Jackson _____ study for his 🧮 test.
3. Lily's mom is a 🩺. She _____ work from Tuesday to Saturday.
4. Addison and I _____ prepare 🍞 🥤 on Saturday mornings.
5. Brianna and her sister _____ walk their 🐕 🐕 every night.
6. Zach _____ take out the 🗑 after school.

**5 Write sentences using *be going to*.**

1. My grandmother / go to the park / tomorrow

_____

2. Ben / watch a movie / tonight

_____

3. The students / visit a museum / next week

_____

4. Sarah and I / do the dishes / after dinner

_____

5. I / clean my room / on Saturday morning

_____

6. You / take out the trash / after lunch

_____

**6 Unscramble the questions.**

1. are / What / you / do / on the weekend / going to / ?

_____

2. you / go / When / on vacation / going to / are / ?

_____

3. going to / your homework / tonight / do / you / Are / ?

_____

**7 In your notebook, answer the questions in Activity 6.**

# Just for Fun

**1** Write sentences in your notebook using *be going to*.

0 Alice

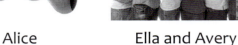

1 Ella and Avery

2 Connor

0. *Alice is going to play video games.*

3 William

4 Julia

5 Keira and John

**2** Write four words for emotions in the first grid. Then play Battleship™ with a classmate!

|   | A | B | C | D | E | F | G | H | I | J |
|---|---|---|---|---|---|---|---|---|---|---|
| 1 | | | | | | | | | | |
| 2 | | | | | | | | | | |
| 3 | | | | | | | | | | |
| 4 | | | | | | | | | | |
| 5 | | | | | | | | | | |
| 6 | | | | | | | | | | |
| 7 | | | | | | | | | | |
| 8 | | | | | | | | | | |
| 9 | | | | | | | | | | |
| 10 | | | | | | | | | | |

|   | A | B | C | D | E | F | G | H | I | J |
|---|---|---|---|---|---|---|---|---|---|---|
| 1 | | | | | | | | | | |
| 2 | | | | | | | | | | |
| 3 | | | | | | | | | | |
| 4 | | | | | | | | | | |
| 5 | | | | | | | | | | |
| 6 | | | | | | | | | | |
| 7 | | | | | | | | | | |
| 8 | | | | | | | | | | |
| 9 | | | | | | | | | | |
| 10 | | | | | | | | | | |

**3** Circle one extra word in each line. Then use the words to form a mystery question.

**ZOE:** Mom, I'm going to watch what a movie with my friends tonight.

**MOM:** You can't go out, Zoe. You are have to study for the geography test, remember?

**ZOE:** Oh, no! But all my friends are you going to watch *A Night with the Zombies*, and I really want to see it!

**MOM:** I understand you're going angry, but your obligations come first.

**ZOE:** OK… And do I have to do to the dishes after dinner?

**MOM:** Of course! It's part of your do chores.

**ZOE:** I hate to take on out the trash.

**MOM:** And I don't like cooking, but I do it every the evening.

**ZOE:** All right… I'm going to talk to Jenny. Weekend maybe we can go together on Sunday.

Mystery question: _____

# Unit 1

## Vocabulary – Sports

**1** Read and write the name of the sport.

~~basketball~~   cycling   rugby   running   soccer   swimming

0. 2 teams / a basket / an orange ball — _basketball_
1. individual / a swimming pool / optional: a stopwatch — _____
2. 2 teams / 15 players per team / 1 ball / no protection / UK, France — _____
3. individual / a bike / a helmet / a stopwatch — _____
4. 2 teams / 11 players per team / a large ball — _____
5. individual / a special track, a park or street — _____

## Adjectives

**2** Unscramble the adjectives.

0. staf — _fast_
1. dlo — _____
2. gbi — _____
3. avecti — _____
4. lalt — _____
5. parupol — _____

**3** Write sentences using the adjectives.

0. _Basketball is a fast_ _____ sport.
1. _____ sport.
2. _____ person.
3. _____ person.
4. _____ person.
5. _____ sport.

**4** Label the pictures.

~~complicated~~   elegant   fast   heavy   ~~tall~~   strong

0. _tall_

1. _____

2. _____

3. _____

4. _____

5. _____

## Ordinal numbers

**5 Match.**

1st — first
2nd — second
3rd — third
4th — fourth
5th — fifth

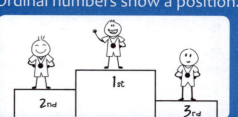

**Guess What!**
Ordinal numbers show a position.

## Grammar – Comparatives

**1 Complete the sentences about you and your friends or family.**

0. I am happier than <u>my friend Frank</u>.
1. _____ is stronger than me.
2. I am more active than _____.
3. _____ taller than _____.
4. _____ more interesting than _____.
5. _____ bigger than _____.
6. _____ heavier than _____.

**Guess What!**
Spelling changes:
heavy ⟶ heavier than
big ⟶ bigger than

**2 Look and write comparisons.**

A

B

0. (old) <u>Bike A is older than bike B.</u>
1. (fast) _____
2. (original) _____
3. (big) _____
4. (modern) _____
5. (tall) _____
6. (popular) _____

# Unit 1

## Superlatives

**3** Find the adjectives. Circle with gray or blue.

- that use *–est*
- that use *the most*

active   big   expensive   fast   heavy   large
modern   old   ~~popular~~   strong   ~~tall~~

| L | A | R | G | E | A | C | G | P | N | F |
|---|---|---|---|---|---|---|---|---|---|---|
| G | H | T | S | W | W | N | B | E | R | A |
| R | A | L | U | P | O | P | X | U | E | S |
| E | Q | Z | H | R | D | P | W | T | D | T |
| U | P | A | T | E | E | B | A | K | O | L |
| X | V | S | E | N | A | L | K | J | M | E |
| Z | Z | X | S | V | L | V | M | D | Z | M |
| K | E | I | J | Z | I | W | Y | O | L | E |
| U | V | F | F | H | B | T | H | N | B | O |
| E | J | A | S | U | C | P | C | G | I | B |
| Q | E | Q | M | Q | S | T | B | A | I | L |

**4** Correct the sentences.

Today I am at the gym with my father and my grandfather.

0. My father is the ~~stronger.~~
   <u>My father is the strongest.</u>

1. My grandpa is the older.
   _____

2. My dad is the happier person in this picture.
   _____

3. I have the nicer hair!
   _____

4. My dad has the big muscles.
   _____

5. I am the shorter of the three.
   _____

## Review

**1** Complete about you!

0. Who has the largest hands in your family? <u>My grandpa has the largest hands.</u>
1. Who is your shortest friend? _____
2. Who has the longest legs in your family? _____
3. Who is your oldest friend? _____
4. Who is the most elegant person in your family? _____
5. Who is the most musical person in your family? _____

## Reading

**1 Read the article and label the pictures.**

Joshua   Leon

### SKATEBOARDING

Skateboarding is a popular activity. There are an estimated 11 million skateboarders around the world! Children, teens and <u>adults</u> can go to a skate park to <u>practice</u> their sport and make new friends. Meet two skateboarders: Joshua and Leon.

Joshua is 15. He likes skateboarding, but he doesn't think it's a sport. Joshua rides his skateboard to school. His friend Leon likes to jump and do <u>tricks</u> with his skateboard. Leon always uses protection to avoid <u>accidents</u> and <u>injuries</u>.

**2 Use red or green to circle the underlined words in the article.**

green: I understand
red: I don't understand

**3 Label the picture.**

skateboarder
skateboard
protection

**4 Write two of the underlined words that correspond.**

_____ n, a special or difficult action that a person performs to impress others: *The skateboarder did _____ in the park.*

_____ n, a grown-up, a fully grown person 21 years or older: *Four children and an _____ are looking at the skateboarder.*

## Writing

**5 Follow the instructions.**

1. Read Julia's and Austin's paragraphs about parkour on page 19.
2. Write a paragraph in your notebook. Express your opinion about skateboarding or parkour: *is it a sport? Is it dangerous?*

# Unit 2

## Vocabulary – Places in the City

**1** Label the places on the map.

0. _coffee shop_
1. _____
2. _____
3. _____
4. _____
5. _____

## Transportation

**2** Label the pictures and cross out the letters you use.

a a a a b b b c c c e e e e f i i k l l m n n o o p r r r r s s t t u u w y y y

0. _bus_    1. _____    2. _____

**3** Unscramble the remaining letters to label the picture.

5. _____    6. _____

___ ___ ___ ___ ___

4 **Circle the correct options.**

0. You need 💲 to **ride a bike** / **take a taxi**.
1. You need to wear a 🪖 to **ride a motorcycle** / **take a bus**.
2. You need to wear a 🔒 to **ride in a car** / **take a train**.
3. You need to wear a ⛑ to **ride a bike** / **take the subway**.
4. You can't have 🍼 with you when you take a **taxi** / **plane**.
5. A driver needs a 🔑 to **ride a motorcycle** / **take the subway**.

## Grammar – Imperatives

1 **Unscramble the letters to complete the directions.**

0. ___Walk___ straight ahead for four blocks.
   lawk

1. _____ past the mall.
   nod't og

2. _____ left on Milford Avenue.
   rutn

3. _____ Triple Oak Park.
   sorsc

4. Oak Coffee Shop is on the _____.
   tihrg

2 **Correct the directions to match the route on the map.**

0. _Walk straight ahead for two_
   _blocks._

1. _____
   _____

2. _____
   _____

3. _____
   _____

4. _____
   _____

131

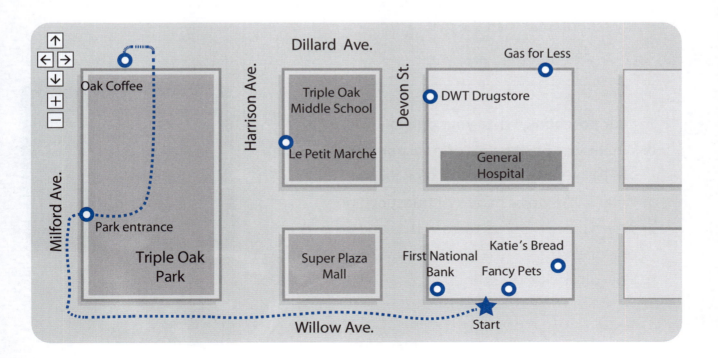

# Unit 2

**Irregular Comparatives and Superlatives**

**3 Circle the correct words to complete the opinions.**

0. Walking to school is (good) / better, but riding my bike to school is (better than) / the best walking.

1. The mall is **better than** / **the best** place in the city! My friends and I hang out there every weekend!

2. My house is **far** / **farther** from school, but my best friend's house is **farther than** / **the farthest** mine.

3. The mall is **worse than** / **the worst** place to hang out with friends in the city. It's soooo boring…

4. Taking a bus in rush hour is **bad** / **worse**, but walking back home from school is **worse than** / **the worst** taking the bus.

## Review

**1 Correct the sentences.**

0. You can buy medicine at a park.
   <u>You can buy medicine at a drugstore.</u>

1. You can buy a soda at a bank.
   _____
   _____

2. My school is far than the mall.
   _____
   _____

3. You can buy vegetables at a school.
   _____
   _____

4. Walk straight and cross left at the hospital.
   _____
   _____

**2 In your notebook, write your opinion.**

0. What is the best means of transportation?
   <u>The best means of transportation is the bus.</u>

1. What is the worst means of transportation?

2. Which place is better to go with friends: a park or a mall?

3. How do you get to school?

> **Guess What!**
> **Ways to go to school:**
> I take the bus/train/subway.
> I take the school bus.
> I ride my bike.
> I walk.
> My mom/dad drives me.

## Reading

**1 Look at the text below. Mark (✓) the correct option.**

1. It's an article. ☐    2. It's an interview. ☐

### What's On? Chronopolis–Celebrity Edition!

**MATT:** This week's celebrity: Sheila Roddick–actress, singer and reality show host. Welcome, Sheila.

**SHEILA:** Hi, Matt. I'm happy to be here, in my own city!

**MATT:** Tell me, do you like living in Chronopolis?

**SHEILA:** Yes, I do. It's a fantastic place.

**MATT:** In your opinion, (0) _what's the best place_ in the city?

**SHEILA:** It's Awesome Coffee. I simply love their cappuccinos. They're so creamy!

**MATT:** Awesome Coffee definitely has lots of fans around here… and what's the (1) _____?

**SHEILA:** Hmm… this a little embarrassing… It's hard for me to say… but I guess it's Green Park.

**MATT:** Green Park? But (2) _____ in Chronopolis?

**SHEILA:** There are too many ducks there… and I'm terrified of ducks.

**MATT:** Oh… I see. And (3) _____?

**SHEILA:** I like it a lot! Actually, I go shopping there two or three times a week. I always need new clothes for my concerts, you know…

**MATT:** Nice! And what's (4) _____ at the mall?

**SHEILA:** Fabulous Fashion is my favorite. The owner is my best friend.

**2 Complete the text with the questions below.**

~~what's the best place~~    why is it the worst place    worst place in town
do you like the X-Mall    your favorite store

## Writing

**3 Look at the map in Activity 2 on page 32. In your notebook, write directions to two places.**

# 3 Unit

## Vocabulary – Physical Description

**1** Use the words from the box to complete the mind maps.

> blue   braces   brown   ~~chubby~~   dark   glasses   green
> medium height   medium weight   short   tall   thin

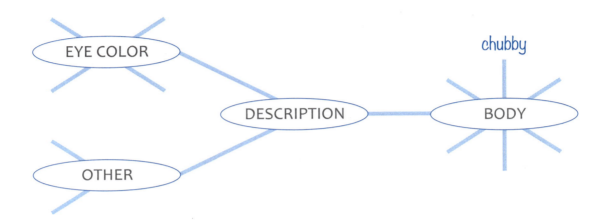

**2** Circle the correct option. Then write the name of the movie.

0. ELSA: I **am** / **(have)** blond hair, but my sister Anna **is** / **has** brown hair. We both **are** / **have** blue eyes. _____Frozen_____

1. MARGO: I **am** / **have** tall and thin. I **am** / **have** brown eyes and hair, and I **am** / **wear** glasses. My little sister Agnes **is** / **has** black hair. My father Gru **is** / **has** tall and **is** / **has** a big nose. _____

2. HICCUP: I **am** / **have** medium height and thin. I **am** / **have** short brown hair and eyes. My friend Astrid **is** / **has** short and thin and **is** / **has** long blond hair. But my best friend is my dragon Toothless. _____

3. RILEY: I **am** / **have** short and thin. I **am** / **have** blond hair and blue eyes. My parents **are** / **have** brown hair. My mom **is** / **wears** glasses and my father **has** / **is** a mustache. _____

**3** Complete the description. Only copy letters from the same column.

| S | H | ~~E~~ | ~~L~~ | G | R | S | T | N | L | O | Y | ~~E~~ | S | ~~H~~ | A | C | H | U | ~~S~~ | B | Y | . | ~~E~~ | R | ~~/~~ |
|---|---|---|---|---|---|---|---|---|---|---|---|---|---|---|---|---|---|---|---|---|---|---|---|---|---|
| A | ~~N~~ | D |   | I | A | E | E | A | ~~A~~ | E | ~~B~~ | D | N | . | ~~I~~ | ~~S~~ | R |   | B | ~~I~~ | ~~N~~ | ~~G~~ |   |   |   |
| ~~S~~ | ~~D~~ | E |   | ~~H~~ | ~~S~~ | ~~I~~ | ~~S~~ | B | L | ~~I~~ | N | A | ~~I~~ | ~~T~~ |   | I | ~~H~~ |   |   |   |   |   |   |   |   |
| A | H | ~~E~~ |   | ~~E~~ |   |   |   |   |   | ~~R~~ |   | D |   |   |   |   |   |   |   |   |   |   |   |   |   |

| A | D | E | L | E |   | I | S |   | A |   | B | R | I | T | I | S | H |   | S | I | N | G | E | R | . |
|---|---|---|---|---|---|---|---|---|---|---|---|---|---|---|---|---|---|---|---|---|---|---|---|---|---|
| S |   |   |   |   |   | S |   |   | L |   |   |   |   |   |   |   | U |   |   |   |   |   |   |   |   |
|   |   | E |   | H |   |   |   | B |   |   |   |   |   | H |   |   |   |   |   |   |   |   |   |   |   |
|   |   | N |   |   |   |   |   |   | E |   |   |   |   |   |   |   |   |   |   |   |   |   |   |   |   |

**Personality**

**4 Complete the words using a, e, i, o, u and y.**

0. _o_ _u_ tg _o_ _i_ ng
1. k __ nd
2. f __ nn __
3. r __ d __
4. s __ r __ __ __ s
5. __ nt __ ll __ g __ nt
6. sh __

**5 Read the review and complete the sentences.**

funny   intelligent   outgoing   popular   shy

**New TV Show Starts on Monday on Channel 7**

*Adventures at the Mall* is about a group of five friends who hang out at the city mall almost every day! Meet the characters in the first season of the series:

Avery is the oldest. She loves to talk and she makes new friends easily.

Arianna tells jokes all the time.

Brandon is Avery's little brother. He always helps his friends and family.

Julia is quiet. She is in love with Brandon, but he doesn't know.

Carter is the geek. He's really into technology and has the best grades at school.

0. Avery is ____outgoing____.
1. Arianna is _____.
2. Brandon is _____.
3. Julia is _____.
4. Carter is _____.

**6 Write your opinions.**

0. My mother is ____funny____.
1. I like people who are _____ and _____.
2. I don't like people who are _____ and _____.
3. My friend is _____.
4. My friends say I'm _____.

# Unit 3

## Grammar – Present Simple

**1** Circle the correct words.

MR. DALE: Marianne, **(do)** / **does** you **has** / **have** a best friend?

MARIANNE: Yes, I **do** / **does**. Riley is my best friend.

MR. DALE: I see. And what **do** / **does** you **do** / **does** together?

MARIANNE: Well… we **listen** / **listens** to music and **studies** / **study** French.

MR. DALE: Nice… now, about the summer program. Why **do** / **does** you **want** / **wants** to participate?

MARIANNE: I **want** / **wants** to spend a month in Québec because I **love** / **loves** the language.

MR. DALE: And **do** / **does** your parents **oppose** / **opposes** the idea?

MARIANNE: Oh, no, they **doesn't** / **don't**. Actually, they are very enthusiastic about it.

MR. DALE: That's great! Thanks, Marianne.

## Present Continuous

**2** Write questions and answers using present continuous.

0. What / Riley / do / now / ?
   <u>What is Riley doing now?</u>
   study / French
   <u>She's studying French.</u>

1. Chloe / study / French / too / ?
   _____
   No
   _____

2. you / wear / a uniform / ?
   _____
   Yes
   _____

3. Where / you / walk / ?
   _____
   walk / to / school
   _____

4. Bob / play / video games / ?
   _____
   No / he / watch / TV
   _____

## Review

**1** Answer about you and a friend in your notebook.

1. What is your friend's name?
2. What does your friend look like?
3. What do you and your friend do together?
4. Does your friend play soccer?
5. Mention one thing where your friend is different from you.

## Reading

**1 Read the text. Then mark (✓) *Manga* and/or *Anime*.**

### Manga and Anime

*Manga* are comics from Japan. Manga comics have a unique style that is easy to recognize:

- There are manga comics for children, teenagers and adults.
- Manga comics are usually printed in black and white.
- Characters in manga comics usually have very big eyes and a small mouth.
- Some manga comics are very long—they can have over 500 pages!

*Anime* is a Japanese word. Anime are animated film productions from Japan (the word is an abbreviation of *animation*). Like manga, anime productions are easy to recognize:

- Many anime productions originate from manga comics.
- There are anime productions for children, teenagers and adults.
- Characters in anime movies also have very big eyes and a very small mouth. Anime characters often have strange hair colors, such as blue and purple!
- The stories are usually more complex than stories in Western animated films. Plots mix real-life topics and fantasy.

|  | Manga | Anime |
|---|---|---|
| 0. Its characters have exaggerated facial characteristics. | ✓ | ✓ |
| 1. Its characters' hair color is usually strange. | ☐ | ☐ |
| 2. It can have many pages. | ☐ | ☐ |
| 3. Its stories combine real and unreal topics. | ☐ | ☐ |
| 4. It is not colored. | ☐ | ☐ |
| 5. People of all ages read or watch it. | ☐ | ☐ |

## Writing

**2 Create your own character. Copy the table in your notebook.**

| Name: _____ | Type (circle): **manga / anime** | Draw your character here. |
|---|---|---|
| Physical characteristics: | | |
| Personality traits: | | |

# Unit 4

## Vocabulary – Food and Drinks

**1** Look at the pictures and solve the puzzle. What is the mystery food?

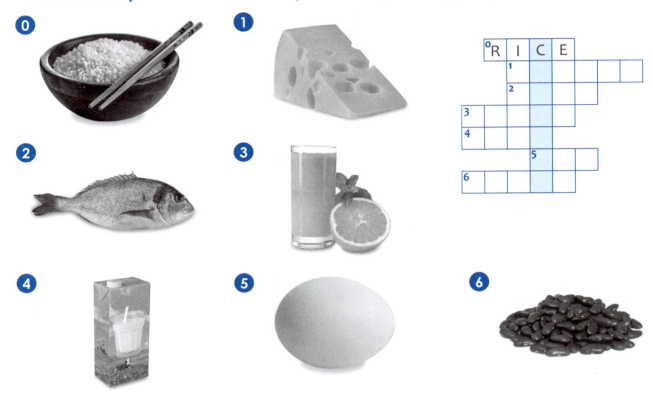

**2** Circle the word that does not belong.

| 0. oranges | apples | (potatoes) | bananas |
|---|---|---|---|
| | | *Potatoes aren't fruit.* | |
| 1. onion | tomatoes | broccoli | fish |
| 2. pasta | milk | butter | cheese |
| 3. beef | rice | chicken | beans |
| 4. soda | juice | water | bread |
| 5. apple | banana | onion | orange |

**3** Write the words in the chart.

beef  broccoli  ~~milk~~  orange juice  water

PLANT PRODUCTS | DRINKS | milk | ANIMAL PRODUCTS

## Grammar – Countable and Uncountable Nouns

**1 Classify the food in the table.**

| Separate ingredients we can count (Countable Nouns) | Mass ingredients we need to measure (Uncountable Nouns) |
|---|---|
| apple | |

**2 Mark the underlined words C (countable) or U (uncountable).**

0. __C__ My sister loves <u>apples</u>.
1. _____ Did you eat six <u>cookies</u>? That's not good for you.
2. _____ People cook <u>potatoes</u> in many different ways.
3. _____ My father puts a lot of <u>butter</u> on his bread.
4. _____ Do you like <u>broccoli</u>?
5. _____ I love a nice salad with <u>tomatoes</u>.
6. _____ Can you give me an <u>orange</u>?

## Some and Any

**3 Read and draw.**

There aren't any apples on the table, but there is one orange. There are some bananas and there is some salad. There aren't any tomatoes. There is some pasta and there is a glass of water.

# 4 Unit

**4** Look. Then write sentences with *some* or *any*.

0. bananas <u>There are some bananas.</u>
   broccoli <u>There isn't any broccoli.</u>
1. eggs _____
2. milk _____
3. tomatoes _____
4. juice _____
5. carrots _____
6. soda _____

**5** Complete the conversations with *some*, *any*, *a* or *an*.

0. A: Do we have __any__ pasta?
   B: Yes, we do, but we don't have __any__ tomatoes to make the sauce.
1. A: Do you want _____ apple for dessert?
   B: Yes, please. And _____ strawberries, too.
2. A: I usually eat _____ cereal and drink _____ juice for breakfast.
   B: Well, I prefer to eat _____ bread with butter, but I don't drink _____ juice.
3. A: We have _____ banana, _____ flour and _____ butter. Let's make a banana mug cake!
   B: Hmm… but we don't have _____ sugar. And we don't have _____ baking soda either.

## Review

**1** Look at the illustration and correct the sentences in your notebook.

0. There are any bananas.
   <u>There aren't any bananas.</u>
1. There aren't any apple.
2. We can see any tomatoes.
3. We can't see some oranges.
4. There are some broccoli.
5. There is any garlic.

## Reading

**1 Read the recipe quickly. Then circle the correct option.**

0. It's a recipe for a type of **cake** / **sandwich**.
1. A **fruit** / **vegetable** is the main ingredient.
2. The tablet shows the **ingredients** / **directions**.

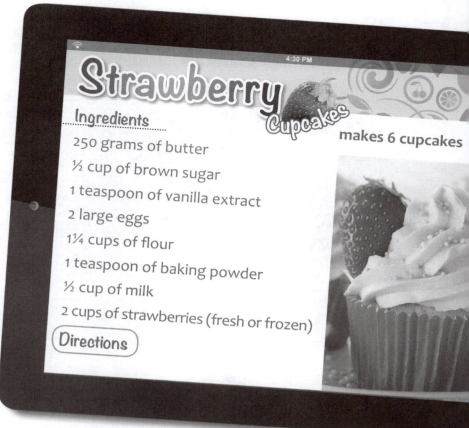

makes 6 cupcakes

**2 Complete the shopping list for 12 cupcakes.**

Hi Mom!
I want to make 12 cupcakes when I get home from school.
We have milk and strawberries. Can you buy the other ingredients, please?
I need:

| | |
|---|---|
| baking powder | 0. 2 teaspoons |
| butter | 1. _____ |
| eggs | 2. _____ |
| flour | 3. _____ |
| vanilla extract | 4. _____ |
| sugar | 5. _____ |

Love,
Morgan

## Writing

**3 Think of your favorite recipe or dish. Write a shopping list for it in your notebook.**

# Unit 5

## Vocabulary – Tourist Attractions

**1** Write the names of the tourist attractions.

0. _amusement park_
1. _____
2. _____
3. _____
4. _____
5. _____
6. _____
7. _____

## Adjectives

**2** Write adjectives from the unit using the letters in the box. Then answer.

```
A B E
F G I L
N O R S
  T U Y
```

0. _interesting_
1. _____
2. _____
3. _____
4. _____
5. _____

Which adjective from the lesson can't you write? _____

**3 Match the comments.**

0. "The amusement park is boring." — ☐ "Yes, I do. Surfing is great there."
1. "Do you like Mango Beach?" — ☐0 "Yeah, it's not interesting at all."
2. "The street market is so noisy!" — ☐ "Yes, too many people want to see the dolphins."
3. "The new art museum is very interesting." — ☐ "It sure is! The old paintings attract a lot of visitors."
4. "The City Aquarium is really crowded." — ☐ "Yes, the **vendors** shout a lot."
5. "The buildings in the historic center are terrible." — ☐ "I agree. The government doesn't protect them."

## Grammar – Verb *be*: *Was, Were*

**1 Complete the sentences using *was* or *were*.**

0. Logan and his friends _____were_____ in the mountains last weekend.
1. The art museum _____ open on Monday.
2. The **vendors** at the street market _____ happy with the tourists' shopping.
3. Riley _____ tired after going to the amusement park yesterday.
4. The **waves** _____ great for surfing at Mango Beach on Sunday.
5. Our visit to the historic center _____ boring.
6. I _____ happy to see the dolphins at the City Aquarium.

**2 Mark the sentences correct (✓) or incorrect (✗). Rewrite the incorrect sentences.**

0. I were at the City Aquarium on Sunday. ✗
   _I was at the City Aquarium on Sunday._

1. Andrew was at the street market yesterday. ☐

   _____

2. Mel and Julia wasn't at the beach on Saturday. ☐

   _____

3. We wasn't at the street market on Monday. ☐

   _____

4. The tourists was interested in the art museum. ☐

   _____

5. Were Alex at the zoo on Tuesday? ☐

   _____

6. Were Caleb and Jayden at the amusement park on Friday? ☐

   _____

**G**lossary

**vendor:** a person that sells a product or service on the street

**wave**

# Unit 5

### 3 Rewrite the sentences using the information in parentheses.

0. You were at the aquarium yesterday.
   (?) <u>Were you at the aquarium yesterday?</u>

1. The old art museum was on Baker Street.
   (-) _____

2. Was the beach polluted last year?
   (-) _____

3. The tigers at the City Zoo weren't hungry.
   (+) _____

4. Alyssa was interested in the historic center.
   (?) _____

5. Were the tourists happy at the street market?
   (+) _____

### 4 In your notebook, write sentences using information from the table.

| Changes in Springville |  |  |
|---|---|---|
|  | **Nowadays** | **In the past** |
| 0. The art museum | open on Mondays | not open on Mondays |
| 1. The historic center | great | terrible |
| 2. The beaches | clean | polluted |
| 3. The amusement park | good for kids | bad for kids |
| 4. The street market | a tourist attraction | not a tourist attraction |

0. Nowadays, the art museum is open on Mondays. <u>In the past, it wasn't open on Mondays.</u>
1. The historic center is great. In the past…
2. The beaches are clean now. In the past…
3. The amusement park is good for kids. In the past…
4. The street market is a tourist attraction now. In the past…

## Review

### 1 In your notebook, answer the questions.

1. What are some tourist attractions in your town or city?
2. Do you like amusement parks?
3. Where were you yesterday?
4. When were you at a zoo?

Blog    Countries    Photos    Contact

### Reading

**1 Read the blog post and number the pictures.**

# TEEN Globetrotter

By Ethan Stewarts

Welcome to the Teen **Globetrotter** blog! Today's post is about my trip to Paris.
(0) Paris is the capital of France.
(1) I was there for a week in July.
My cousin Leo and I were at all the famous places. (2) A sightseeing bus tour was the start of our trip.
We were at the Eiffel Tower, and the **view** was amazing. (3) My cousin was great in the picture with the tower!
We were also at the Louvre, a very big and interesting museum. (4) But there were many people, and there was a terrible line to buy tickets!
The *Arc de Triomphe* is another famous tourist attraction. Fortunately, (5) the streets around it weren't very crowded.

[continue reading]

### Writing

**2 Write a blog post about a tourist attraction using *was* and *were*.**

_____
_____
_____
_____

**Glossary**
**globetrotter:** a person who travels a lot
**view:** panorama

# Unit 6

## Vocabulary – Movie and Book Genres

**1** Label the movie and book genres.

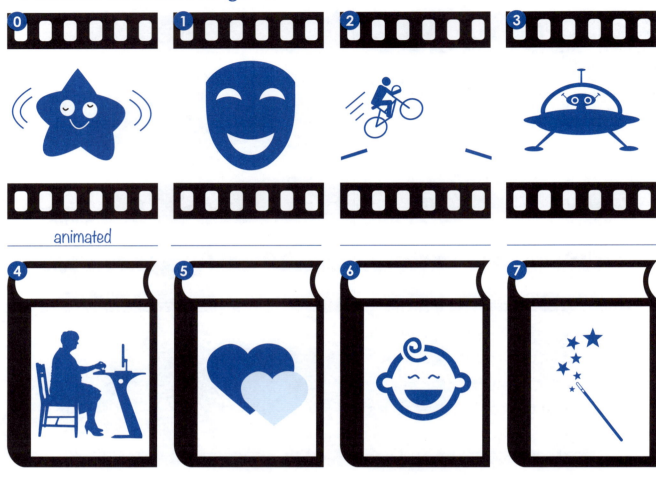

0. animated
1. 
2. 
3. 
4. 
5. 
6. 
7. 

**2** Match the sentences.

0. Do you like action movies?
1. Do you read autobiographies?
2. Who is your favorite romance book author?
3. What were your favorite children's books?
4. How often do you watch science-fiction movies?
5. What was the last comedy movie you saw?
6. What is your favorite fantasy book?

☐ Yes, I do. I'm reading *I Am Malala* right now.
[0] No, I don't. They are too violent for me.
☐ Stephenie Meyer is my favorite. The *Twilight* series is really good.
☐ I watch them every weekend. It's my favorite movie genre.
☐ *The Hobbit!* J.R.R. Tolkien is a great author.
☐ I liked fairy tales, such as *Cinderella* and *Little Red Riding Hood*.
☐ I saw *Fun with The Spencers* yesterday. It was really funny!

## Adjectives

**3 Complete the sentences using the adjectives.**

boring   funny   ~~inspirational~~   interesting   sad

0. __Inspirational__ books make readers want to change their lives, or even the world.
1. _____ movies can make people fall asleep at the movie theater.
2. _____ books capture readers' attention. It is difficult to stop reading them.
3. _____ movies can make people cry.
4. _____ movies usually make people feel happy. They laugh a lot.

## Grammar – Past Simple

**1 Categorize the verbs.**

cry   like   love   play   start   study   work

| Verb | Verb ending in e |
|---|---|
| want → want**ed** | create → creat**ed** |
| _____ → _____ | _____ → _____ |
| _____ → _____ | _____ → _____ |

Regular Verbs in Past

| Verb ending in vowel + y | Verb ending in consonant + y |
|---|---|
| stay → stay**ed** | try → tr**ied** |
| _____ → _____ | _____ → _____ |
|  | _____ → _____ |

**2 Read and circle the correct verbs.**

When I was little, I **(liked)** / **played** to visit my grandfather David. He is an expert storyteller and he always **crashed** / **created** his own adventure stories. I loved the stories, and I always **wanted** / **worked** a new one. Sometimes I laughed and sometimes I **created** / **cried**.
Yesterday I **asked** / **worked** my grandpa to write or dictate his stories on the computer. He said, "When they **publish** / **study** my book, you get 50%!"

Grandpa David & me

## 6 Unit

**3 Circle the irregular verbs and write them in the table.**

~~go~~   live   make   meet   see   start   study   visit   write

| Present | Past |
|---|---|
| go | went |
|   |   |
|   |   |
|   |   |
|   |   |

**4 Complete the sentences using the past simple. Then circle T (True) or F (False).**

0. Saint-Exupéry ___made___ (make) the illustrations for
   The Little Prince.  **(T)**  F
1. Roald Dahl _____ (meet) Saint-Exupéry in Africa
   and they became friends.  T  F
2. Dahl and Saint-Exupéry _____ (live) in Europe and
   in America.  T  F
3. Dahl _____ (go) on a mission in his plane
   and disappeared.  T  F
4. Roald Dahl _____ (create) The Gremlins.  T  F
5. Saint-Exupéry _____ (write) The Little Prince in
   250 languages.  T  F

### Review

**1 Correct the sentences using the past simple.**

0. My family and I seed a great movie last night.
   _My family and I saw a great movie last night._
1. It were about zombies that live in an Italian city.
   _____
2. A scientist finded a medicine that make the zombies sleepy.
   _____
3. The special effects where really scary. I want to close my eyes.
   _____

## Reading

# Edgar Allan Poe

a raven

The American writer Edgar Allan Poe wrote mystery and horror stories. He was born in Boston, in the US, in 1809. After his mother died, he was adopted by a nice family. "Allan" was the name of his adoptive parents.

People call Poe "The Father of the Detective Story" because he started this genre of stories. He worked for magazines and newspapers, and he wrote many short stories and poems. Poe died in mysterious conditions: he was in another man's clothes!

### 1 Complete the sentences with When or After that.

1. _____ Edgar's mother died, he was adopted.
2. _____, his name was Edgar *Allan* Poe.
3. _____ he died, he was 40 years old.

## Writing

### 2 In your notebook, write about Edgar Allan Poe. Also use *Then*.

1809 – born
1812 – mother died, adopted
1926 – to university
1836 – married cousin Virginia
1845 – published "The Raven": famous poem
1849 – died

Edgar Allan Poe was born in 1809. When his mother died, …

# Unit 7

## Vocabulary – Professions and Workplaces

**1** Solve the crossword puzzle.
Write the professions.

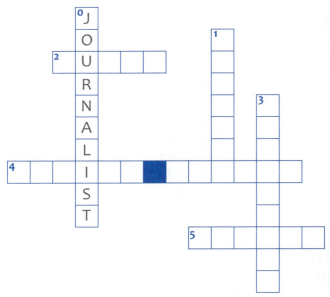

**2** Circle the correct professions.

0. Some **nurses** / **scientists** administer medication.
1. **Social workers** / **Teachers** help people learn about a subject.
2. **Journalists** / **Artists** collect information and present it on TV or on the Internet.
3. **Social workers** / **Nurses** help people solve personal problems.
4. Some **teachers** / **artists** paint, and others make music.
5. Some **scientists** / **journalists** work in labs and teach at universities.

**3** Complete the sentences using the words below.

community centers   hospitals   laboratories   offices   ~~schools~~   studios

0. Teachers usually work at _schools_.
1. Nurses typically work at _____.
2. Most scientists work at _____.
3. Social workers can work at _____.
4. Artists frequently work at _____.
5. Journalists can work at _____.

## Grammar – Past Simple

**1 Complete the questions in past tense using the verbs in parentheses.**

File | Edition | Show | Favorites | Tools | Help

*Teens do very important jobs in Help the **Elderly**. Let's meet Alex Park.*

### Past Simple, Negative

Jo **didn't play** football yesterday.
(didn't) (verb)

**HE:** Alex, when did you join _____ (join) *Help the Elderly?*

**ALEX:** I joined last year.

**HE:** Why (1) _____ (become) a volunteer?

**ALEX:** Because I wanted to help in our community. Now I take elderly people shopping at the supermarket.

**HE:** What (2) _____ (do) in the beginning?

**ALEX:** I worked in the library at the community center.

**HE:** (3) _____ (receive) any training?

**ALEX:** Yes, I did.

**HE:** (4) What _____ (learn) in the training?

**ALEX:** I learned how to work with elderly people. I like them a lot. They tell cool stories!

**2 Reread the text on page 100. Mark the statements T (True) or F (False). Then rewrite the incorrect sentences.**

1. Zach joined GoGreen when he was 9.   T   F

   _____

2. He met a GoGreen volunteer at a park.   T   F

   _____

3. Zach didn't plant trees when he joined GoGreen.   T   F

   _____

4. He took some classes about plants.   T   F

   _____

5. He didn't like helping other volunteers.   T   F

   _____

**G**lossary
**elderly:** senior, somewhat old

# Unit 7

**3** Read about Anne Sullivan. Then read the sentences below and correct them in your notebook.

Anne Sullivan was born in 1866, in the United States. She got her first job when she was 21, and she moved to Alabama. She was Helen Keller's teacher, a **blind** and **deaf** girl. She taught Keller to communicate. Later on, she helped Keller study at Radcliffe College, a university in Cambridge, Massachusetts. They also traveled together around the United States, where they met famous people such as Alexander Graham Bell and Thomas Edison. Anne Sullivan died on October 20, 1936.

0. Anne Sullivan got her first job when she was 14.
   *Anne Sullivan didn't get her first job when she was 14. She got her first job when she was 21.*
1. She taught Helen Keller to play the piano.
2. She helped Keller study at primary school.
3. She traveled with Keller around the world.
4. Anne Sullivan died in 1836.

**4** Read Anne Sullivan's biography again. Then complete the questions.

0. When *did Anne Sullivan get* _____ her first job?
   She got her first job in 1887.
1. Did _____ to New York?
   No, she didn't. She moved to Alabama.
2. How many students _____ ?
   She had only one student, Helen Keller.
3. Where _____ ?
   Helen Keller studied at Radcliffe College, in Massachusetts.
4. What famous people _____ ?
   They met Alexander Graham Bell and Thomas Edison.

| Time Expressions |
| --- |
| *yesterday, two days ago, three weeks ago, last Monday, last weekend, last year* |

## Review

**1** In your notebook, answer the questions.

1. Where did you go last weekend?
2. How many movies did you see last year?
3. Where did you study when you were little?
4. Did you like your elementary school? Why?

**G**lossary

**blind:** (a person that) cannot see

**deaf:** (a person that) cannot hear

## Reading

**1 Read the text. Then mark (✓) the best answer.**

The purpose of the text is to:

a. ☐ *persuade* readers to become volunteers.

b. ☐ *describe* a volunteer to its readers.

c. ☐ *inform* readers about the activities at Springtown Community Center.

### Springtown Community Center needs teen volunteers!

Do you want to…
- share your energy and talent with children?
- feel that you are making the world a better place?
- have fun and help other people?

If you are 12 – 17 years old, you can work as a teen volunteer with us. We need volunteers for:

Sports coaching – Music classes – Art classes – Tutoring

Register at www.springtowncommcenter.org Don't forget to ask your parents for permission to join the program.

## Writing

**2 Number the text about a personal hero.**

☐ Last year, she helped many kids with math.

☐ Ms. Torres is my personal hero because she cares about other people. She inspires me to be a teacher when I'm older!

☐ 1 My neighbor, Ms. Torres, is a teacher.

☐ She taught them after school time. She was fun, very patient and kind.

**3 In your notebook, write about a partner's personal hero. Refer to page 103.**

# 8 Unit

## Vocabulary – Chores and Free-time Activities

**1 Circle the correct words.**

0. My mom hates to **do** / **walk** the dishes.
1. How often do you **clean** / **walk** your dog?
2. Melissa and her cousins **go** / **watch** movies every weekend.
3. I don't usually **do** / **go** to the park.
4. Do you want to **clean** / **do** your room now?
5. Sometimes Landon and I **go** / **hang out** with our friends after school.
6. My neighbors always **play** / **take out** the trash in the morning.
7. I can **clean** / **play** video games after doing my homework.

**2 Classify the activities from Activity 1.**

| Chores | Free-time Activities |
|---|---|
| do the dishes | |
| | |
| | |
| | |

## Emotions

**3 Solve the crossword.**

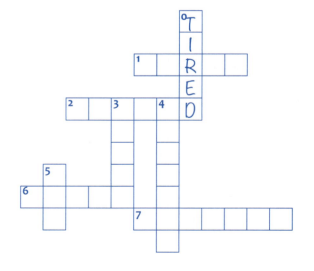

DOWN

0.
3.
4.
5.

ACROSS

1.  2.  6.  7.

**4 How do you feel? Complete the sentences.**

0. I feel _____ bored _____ when I do the dishes.
1. I feel _____ when I play video games.
2. I feel _____ when I fight with a friend.
3. I feel _____ when I get a good grade at school.
4. I feel _____ when I _____.

## Grammar – Have to

**1 Mark the sentences correct (✓) or incorrect (✗). Rewrite the incorrect ones.**

0. My sister have to clean the kitchen after dinner every night. ✗
   My sister has to clean the kitchen after dinner every night.

1. The teachers have to correct the tests to give students the final grade. ☐
   _____

2. Do you have to take out the trash at your house? ☐
   _____

3. We has to do our homework before playing video games. ☐
   _____

4. How often do people have to go to the dentist? ☐
   _____

5. Students in Japan has to clean their classrooms. ☐
   _____

**2 Read the chat and write sentences. Use have to or has to.**

0. Owen and John have to buy balloons, paper cups and plates.
1. Hunter _____
   _____
2. Katie _____
   _____
3. Julia and Alex _____
   _____
4. Kim _____
   _____
5. Gabriel and Luke _____
   _____

🛜     4:30 PM     🔋

◀ MESSAGES      EDIT

**Organizing Sean's Party**
Alex, Gabriel, Hunter, John, Julia, Luke, Katie, Kim, …

Hey Guys!
We still have to do lots of things for Sean's surprise birthday party tomorrow! Here are the tasks and the people in charge:
Buy balloons, paper cups and plates: Owen and John
Make the chocolate cake: Hunter
Make fruit juice: Katie
Decorate Kim's garage for the party: Julia and Alex
Prepare playlist: Kim
Distract Sean: Gabriel and Luke
We have to hurry!

# Unit 8

## Future: Going to

**3 Complete the sentences using be going to.**

0. Sean's friends <u>are going to throw</u> (throw) a surprise birthday party for him.
1. Our school _____ (organize) a big video game championship.
2. My parents _____ (travel) this weekend, but I _____ (stay) at my grandparents'.
3. I _____ (watch, neg.) A Night with the Zombies. I was too scared by the trailer!
4. Carter _____ (play, neg.) the guitar in the school band next year.

**4 Write sentences about Anna's plans.**

0. On Monday, <u>Anna is going to play soccer at the park.</u>
1. On Tuesday, _____
_____
2. On Wednesday, _____
_____
3. On Thursday, _____
_____

| | 4:30 PM | |
|---|---|---|
| | Calendar | |
| | ◀ November 2015 ▶ | |
| Mon, Nov 19 | All aft | play soccer at the park |
| Tue, Nov 20 | All aft | study for the history test |
| Wed, Nov 21 | Eve | go to the supermarket with Mom |
| Thu, Nov 22 | All day | help Mom & Dad prepare dinner |

**5 Write questions. Ask about the words in bold.**

0. <u>What are you going to do on the holiday?</u>
I'm going to **travel to the beach** on the holiday.
1. _____
I'm going to travel **with my cousins**.
2. _____
We're going to stay **at a hotel**.
3. _____
Yes, we're going to **travel by bus**.

## Review

**1 In your notebook, answer the questions.**

1. What is your favorite free-time activity?
2. What are you going to do on the weekend?
3. Are you going to travel on your next vacation?
4. What chores do you have to do at home?

## Reading

**1 Read the conversation. Then write T (True) or F (False) and correct the false sentences.**

YUNA: Hey, Natsuki! Would you like to come to my birthday party?
NATSUKI: When is it?
YUNA: It's on Friday, June 24.
NATSUKI: Sure, I'd love to. What time is it?
YUNA: We're going to start at 7 p.m.
NATSUKI: And where is it?
YUNA: At my house.
NATSUKI: Great!
YUNA: It's going to be a costume party, OK?
NATSUKI: A costume party? Wow! Costume parties are fun! What costume are you going to wear?
YUNA: I can't tell you. It's going to be a surprise! Look, here's the invitation.
NATSUKI: Thanks, Yuna. I'm going wear my Temari costume!

0. It's Natsuki's birthday party.　　　　T　(F)
   _It's Yuna's birthday party._

1. The party is going to be on Friday, July 24.　　T　F

2. It's going to be a surprise party.　　T　F

3. Natsuki likes costume parties.　　T　F

4. Yuna is going to dress up like Temari.　　T　F

## Writing

**2 Create an invitation for Yuna's party.**

# Just for Fun Answer Key

## Unit 1
**1** *Clockwise from the top*: the world, soccer, basketball, Christmas, volleyball, baseball, golf, rubber bands
**2** *From top to bottom*: 2, 1, 4, 3
**3** *Down*: 1. traceuse  2. table tennis
*Across*: 3. cycling  4. heaviest  5. sports
**4**

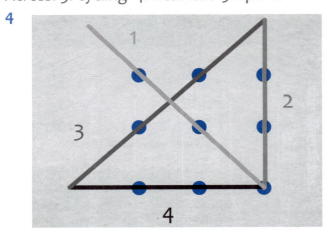

## Unit 2
**1** The missing word is *coffee shop*.
**2** 1. bike  2. car  3. bus  4. taxi
**3** 1. right  2. left  3. Cross  4. Walk  5. Don't
*Secret direction*: Walk straight ahead.
**4** 1. farther  2. best  3. worse  4. farthest
5. better  6. worst

## Unit 3
**1** *Down*: 1. chubby  2. thin  4. tall
*Across*: 2. short  5. long
**2** 1. Jim Parsons  2. Katy Perry  3. Hugh Jackman  4. Emma Watson
**3** intelligent, outgoing, kind, funny

## Unit 4
**1** *Example of correct answers*: apple, beans, butter, carrots, eggs, onion, orange, pasta, rice, water
**2** *Food items*: beans, beef, bread, butter, cheese, eggs, rice, yogurt
**3** Answers will vary.
**4** 1. F: the word *batata* is not Portuguese but Taíno.  2. T  3. F: a chicken can lay 250 eggs a year or more.  4. T

## Unit 5
**1** *Down*: beach, street market, amusement park, zoo
*Across*: art museum, aquarium, mountains, historic center
**2** F; it accommodates 525 passengers.  2. T
3. F: It's Mount Everest in Nepal.  4. T
5. F: The most visited museum in the world is the Louvre in Paris, France.  6. T
**3** Answers will vary.

## Unit 6
**1** autobiography, fantasy, romance, children's, comedy, animated, action
*Mystery genre*: science fiction
**2** One child, one teacher, one book, and one pen can change the world.
**3** *Down*: 1. saw  2. found  4. spoke  5. met
*Across*: 3. wrote  5. made  6. lost  7. went
They are all *irregular* verbs.

## Unit 7
**1** 1. nurse  2. scientist  3. journalist  4. artist
5. teacher  6. social worker
**2** 1. was / were  2. went  3. had  4. made
5. met  6. rode  7. took  8. threw
**3** *Extra words*: 1. do  2. what  3. yesterday
4. did  5. you
*Mystery question*: What did you do yesterday?

## Unit 8
**1** *Example of correct answers*: 1. Ella and Avery are going to hang out with their friends.  2. Connor is going to clean his room.  3. William is going to take out the trash.  4. Julia is going to go to the movies.
5. Keira and John are going to go to the park.
**2** Answers will vary.
**3** *Mystery question*: What are you going to do on the weekend?

# Unit 1

## Comparatives

We use comparatives to talk about the differences between two people, places or things.
- *Kevin is **taller than** George.*
- *A car is **more expensive than** a bicycle.*

When using comparatives, we use short (one syllable) and long (two or more syllables) adjectives.
- *My brother is **tall**.*
- *Those running shoes are **expensive**.*

We form the comparative of short adjectives by adding –er followed by *than*.
- *Carla is **stronger than** Grace.*
- *My brothers are **older than** me.*

We form the comparative of long adjectives by using *more* + adjective + *than*.
- *Soccer is **more interesting than** golf.*
- *Dogs are **more energetic than** turtles.*

For short adjectives ending in a vowel + consonant, double the consonant before adding –er.
- *Miami is **hotter than** New York.*
- *A basketball is **bigger than** a soccer ball.*

If a short adjective ends in a consonant + –y, it becomes –ier in the comparative form.
- *Daniel is **happier than** Evan.*
- *Playing a sport is **healthier than** watching TV.*

## Superlatives

We use superlatives when we compare three or more nouns.
- *Michigan Stadium is **the largest** stadium in the US.*
- *John is **the most athletic** student in our school.*

We form the superlative of short adjectives by adding –est to the adjective.
- *Maria is **the youngest** girl on the basketball team.*
- *We are **the fastest** runners in the competition.*

We form the superlative of long adjectives by using *most* + adjective.
- *Soccer is probably **the most popular** sport in the world.*
- *I think that rugby is **the most dangerous** team sport.*

For short adjectives ending in vowel + consonant, double the consonant before adding –est.
- *What is **the hottest** place on Earth?*
- ***The biggest** trophy is for the winners.*

If a short adjective ends in a consonant + –y, it becomes –iest in the superlative form.
- ***The happiest** time in my life was when I won first prize.*
- *That's **the funniest** joke ever!*

## Imperatives

We use imperatives to give instructions and advice.
- **Drive** straight ahead here.
- **Don't turn** left.

To form imperatives in the affirmative, use only the verb.
- **Cross** through the park and **turn** right.

To form imperatives in negative, use don't + the verb.
- **Don't ride** your skateboard here.

## Irregular Comparatives and Superlatives

There are a number of irregular comparatives. *Good* becomes *better*.
- I think our school is **better than** Chronopolis Middle School.

*Bad* becomes *worse*.
- Coffee at the X-Mall is **worse than** at the Awesome Coffee Shop.

*Far* becomes *farther*.
- The mall is **farther than** the convenience store.

The same adjectives also make irregular superlatives.

*Good* becomes *the best*.
- Our school is **the best** middle school in the city.

*Bad* becomes *the worst*.
- Unique is **the worst** store in the X-Mall; their clothes aren't modern at all.

*Far* becomes *the farthest*.
- Linden Park is in **the farthest** of the three parks in our city.

# 3 Unit

## Present Simple

We use the present simple to talk about routines, repeated actions and general truths.

- A good friend **respects** your differences.

We use the base form of the verb with *I*, *you*, *we* and *they*.

- My friends **help** me with my homework.

We use the third person singular form with *he*, *she* and *it*. To make this form, we add –s or –es to the base form of the verb.

- Gloria **enjoys** cosplay events.
- She **dresses up** as a cartoon character.

To form negative sentences, we add the auxiliary verb *don't* (*doesn't* for *he*, *she*, *it*) and the base form of the verb.

- Betty **doesn't walk** to school.

We form questions with the auxiliary verb *do* (*does* for *he*, *she*, *it*) and the base form of the verb.

- **Do** you **watch** a lot of TV during the week?
- **Does** Mike **play** many video games?

We use Do (Does for *he*, *she*, *it*) for short answers. The main verb is omitted.

- **Do** you **like** popcorn? Yes, I **do**.
- **Does** your brother **play** table tennis? No, he **doesn't**.

We form information questions by adding a Wh– word to the beginning of a Yes/No question.

- **Where do** you **live**?
- **When does** Paul **visit** his grandmother?

## Present Continuous

We use the present continuous to talk about activities that are happening now.

- Peter **is watching** TV.
- They **are listening** to music.

We form the present continuous with the verb *be* in the present simple, and the base form of the verb with –ing.

- My sister **is doing** her homework.
- We **are eating** dinner.

We form the negative by adding *not* (*n't*) after the verb *be*.

- I **am not wearing** new shoes.
- Josh **isn't playing** basketball.

To form questions, we put the verb *be* before the subject.

- **Are** you **watching** a movie?
- **Is** Paula **riding** her skateboard at the park?

We use the verb *be* for short answers to questions in present continuous.

- **Are** you **eating** lunch? Yes, **I am**.
- **Is** Bobby **listening** to music? No, he **isn't**.

To ask for information, we place the Wh– word before the verb *be*.

- **Where are** you **taking** lessons?
- **Why are** they **smiling**?

## Countable and Uncountable Nouns

We use **countable nouns** for separate objects or ingredients that we can count: *tablespoon, mug, banana*.

Countable nouns can be singular or plural. We use the articles *a* and *an* with countable nouns.
- I brought **a sandwich** and **an apple** for lunch.
- There are **five books** on the desk.

We cannot count uncountable nouns. They have no plural form, but it is possible to count them and measure them with weights or volume.
- We need **two cups of flour** to bake the cake.
- After the soccer game, he drank almost **two liters of water**.

## Quantifiers: *some, any*

We use *some* with both countable and uncountable nouns to express a moderate quantity.
- We bought **some apples** at the supermarket.
- Shelley had **some bread** and **some coffee** for breakfast.

In negative sentences, we use *any* with both countable and uncountable nouns.
- There **aren't any oranges** left for desert.
- I don't have **any sugar** for my tea.

We use *any* in questions to ask about the existence of uncountable or plural countable nouns.
- Is there **any milk** left in the fridge?
- Are there **any spoons** on the table?

## Food Containers and Measures

Types of containers are commonly used with countable and uncountable nouns: *bags, boxes, cans, cups, glasses, bottles,* and so on.
- Can I have **two bottles of water**, please?
- I need a **bag of potatoes**.

We use *kilos, cups, teaspoons* (and so on) with measureable countable and uncountable nouns:
- We need one **cup of** oil, a **kilo of** potatoes and a **teaspoon of** pepper.
- Did you get the **two kilos of** beef for the hamburgers?

**Verb *be*: *was*, *were***

The past of the verb *be* takes two forms: *was* or *were*.
- We **were** at the movies yesterday.
- The new Superman movie **was** great.

We form the negative by adding *not*.
- She **was not** in class this morning.
- They **were not** at home last night.

The contracted forms are *wasn't* and *weren't*.
- We **weren't** hungry last night.
- My class in the library **wasn't** boring.

To form Yes/No questions, we put the verb *be* before the subject.
- **Was** he on vacation last week?
- **Were** you happy on your last vacation?

To ask for information, we add a Wh– word to the beginning of a Yes/No question.
- **When was** he on vacation?
- **Where were** you this morning?

We can use the verb *be* with the expression *there* to talk about the existence of places or objects in the past.
- **There was** a big amusement park near the hotel.
- **There were** many people in the historic center.

Some common time expressions used with the past simple are:
- yesterday
- two days ago, three weeks ago
- last Monday, last weekend, last year in 2012, in 1750

## Unit 6

**Past Simple**

We use the past simple to talk about a completed action that took place at a definite moment in the past.
- I **visited** my aunt in California two weeks ago.
- We **studied** English when we were in elementary school.

Verbs in the past simple can be regular or irregular.
- Roald Dahl **published** many books and stories in his life.
- John **went** to the hospital to visit a friend.

Most regular verbs end in –ed in affirmative sentences in the past simple.
- My sister **worked** at the public swimming pool on weekends.
- I **created** a new kind of apple pie!

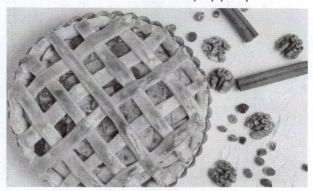

If a regular verb ends in a consonant + –y, it changes to –ied in the past simple.
- I **studied** math last night.
- Paula **cried** because the movie was sad.

Irregular verbs in the past simple take several different forms.
- We **did** a lot of homework this morning.
- Thomas **went** to the supermarket last weekend.

To study the irregular verbs forms, use the Verb List on page 168.

We use the past form of irregular verbs in affirmative sentences.
- Angie **drove** all the way from Los Angeles to San Francisco.
- My aunt **bought** a big red car last Monday.

The past simple uses time expressions that refer to finished periods of time.
- I **heard** a strange noise **last night.**
- We **took** your swimming class **yesterday.**

# Unit 7

## Past Simple (Negative)

Negative sentences use the auxiliary *did* + *not* or *didn't* before the base form of the verb.

- They **did not (didn't) visit** their friends in Paris.

- Miriam **did not (didn't)** play volleyball last year.

## Past Simple (Yes/No Questions)

To form *Yes/No* questions, we put the auxiliary *did* before the subject and use the base form of the verb.

- **Did** you **read** Don Quixote?

- **Did** she **have** lunch with you?

# Unit 8

## Have to

*Have to* expresses obligation.
- Matt **has to** take the dog out for a walk.

In the present simple, we use *has* with the third person.
- John **has to** write a short essay for history class.
- My mom **has to** work late today.

We form Yes/No questions with *have to* by using *Do* or *Does* before the subject.
- **Does** Maria **have to** go to the supermarket today?
- **Do** I **have to** wear a uniform at the Scouts?

## Future with *Going to*

We use *going to* to describe a future plan or make a prediction.
- You**'re going to** interview your classmates today.
- I**'m going to** take a lot of pictures on our trip.

We form the future with *going to* with the auxiliary verb *be* + *going to* + the base form of the verb.
- Jill **is going to get** a new tablet for her birthday.
- They **are going to visit** Rome next month.

The verb *be* is commonly contracted.
- I**'m** going to clean my room.
- We**'re** going to organize the closet together.

To form a negative sentence, we add *not* to the verb *be*. Contractions are possible.
- I **am not (I'm not) going to wash** the windows!
- Class **is not (isn't) going to meet** today.

To form Yes/No questions, we put the verb *be* before the subject.
- **Is** the teacher **going to give** you a good grade for your presentation?
- **Are** you **going to help** me with my homework?

167

# Verb List Irregular verbs

| Present Simple – Past Simple | Study Lists |
|---|---|

**Present Simple – Past Simple**

be – was / were
begin – began
break – broke
build – built
buy – bought
choose – chose
come – came
do – did
draw – drew
drive – drove
eat – ate
fall – fell
feel – felt
find – found
fly – flew
get – got
give – gave
go – went
grow – grew
have – had
hear – heard
know – knew
leave – left
lose – lost
make – made
meet – met
pay – paid
read – read
run – ran
see – saw
sing – sang
speak – spoke
swim – swam
take – took
teach – taught
tell – told
think – thought
wear – wore
win – won

**Completely irregular**
be – was / were
go – went

**With an o in past**
break – broke
choose – chose
drive – drove
get – got
lose – lost
speak – spoke
tell – told
wear – wore
win – won

**With a long –ew sound in past**
fly – flew
grow – grew
draw – drew
know – knew

**With a short e sound in past**
fall – fell
feel – felt
leave – left
meet – met

**Ending in –ought / –aught in past**
buy – bought
teach – taught
think – thought

*i becomes a*
begin – began
give – gave
sing – sang
swim – swam

**Long *a* sound in past**
come – came
eat – ate
make – made
pay – paid

**The others**
build – built
do – did
find – found
have – had
hear – heard
read – read
run – ran
see – saw
take – took